PLANT-BASED
VEGAN MEAT COOKBOOK

Plant-Based VEGAN MEAT COOKBOOK

50 Impossibly Delicious Vegan Recipes Using Meat Substitutes

— HOLLY V. GRAY —

Photography by Antonis Achilleos

ROCKRIDGE
PRESS

For general information on our other products and services or to obtain technical support, please contact our Customer Care Department within the United States at (866) 744-2665, or outside the United States at (510) 253-0500.

Rockridge Press publishes its books in a variety of electronic and print formats. Some content that appears in print may not be available in electronic books, and vice versa.

Interior and Cover Designer: Monica Cheng
Art Producer: Samantha Ulban
Editor: Gurvinder Singh Gandu
Production Editor: Rachel Taenzler
Production Manager: Jose Olivera

Photography © 2021 Antonis Achilleos. Food styling by Rishon Hanners.
Author photo courtesy of milkhoneyphotog.
Cover image: Ground "Beef" Wellington with Mushroom Gravy, page 76.

ISBN: Paperback 978-1-64876-461-5
eBook 978-1-64876-462-2
R0

For my dad, the late Stephen E. Grant,
who instilled in me the value of hospitality
and the power of a great meal
to bring people together.

CONTENTS

INTRODUCTION

The way we define "meat" is evolving.

Sales of vegan meats have been on the rise each year, with projections for vegan meats set to reach a global market share of over $35 billion by 2027. While still a relatively small figure compared to worldwide meat sales overall, this upward trajectory is indicative of consumers' increasing interest in the health benefits of eliminating or reducing animal-based meats from their diets as well as the social issues of climate change and animal rights. And it's not just vegans who are driving these sales.

Vegan meat is becoming an increasingly popular choice among nonvegan and nonvegetarian consumers. Fueled by the explosive growth of brands such as Gardein, Beyond Meat, Sweet Earth, No Evil Foods, Unreal Deli, and Impossible Foods, the vegan meat market receives a large portion of support from nonvegans who are either curious about eliminating meat from their plates entirely or simply wanting to incorporate more meatless meals into their weekly rotation.

I grew up eating meat. I enjoyed all the sensory experiences of eating meat and the deeply ingrained traditions surrounding it. Yet, even as a child, I had the nagging sense that something about it wasn't right for me. I experimented with vegetarianism off and on throughout my teenage years and eventually, as an adult, began to do my own research into factory farming and other issues surrounding meat production. My personal reasons for ditching meat for good actually had nothing to do with the taste.

As a former meat eater (I went vegetarian in 2012 and vegan on New Year's Day 2017), I wanted to write a book that highlights the variety of ways the flavors, textures, and experiences of eating the meats many of us grew up with can be replicated without causing undue harm to ourselves, the planet, or animals.

To clarify, this book is not a how-to guide for making your own vegan meats. That's a whole other topic entirely. Rather, this book is a resource that you can reference for creative and flavorful ways of cooking with brand-name vegan meats.

My personal goal is to ensure that you have success cooking with vegan meats. The way I'm going to do this is by helping you get familiar with the wide array of products available today. Although not every brand or variety of vegan meat is represented in this book, I've kept the ingredients lists to items I have personally observed to be most widely accessible through grocery retailers in major cities across the United States. There's no need to run out and buy any fancy tools or equipment, either. All of the recipes in the book can be made on the stove or in the oven using standard pots, pans, and baking sheets found in the average American kitchen. There's even a recipe for vegan turkey pinwheels that doesn't require cooking at all (see page 13). My hope is that you quickly become at ease with these recipes and that they help make the act of eating vegan meats feel familiar and comfortable in a way that encourages you to experiment with adapting some of your old favorite recipes with a few easy vegan modifications.

The fact that you have picked up a book on vegan meats tells me that you are ready and open to begin the journey of eliminating or reducing animal-based meat from your diet. Or maybe you're already loving the vegan lifestyle and you're looking for more delicious ways to enjoy the growing world of vegan meats on the market today. Whatever path has led you to this book, I'm glad you're here. I hope you enjoy the collection of recipes I've included and that they inspire your own creativity in the kitchen. Welcome! Let's get started!

Pulled "Pork" Hash // p. 65

Chapter 1

THE WORLD OF VEGAN MEATS

Now is an exciting time to dive into the rapidly expanding world of vegan meats. In this chapter, you will find the information you need to get started on your personal journey toward incorporating vegan meats into your weekly meal plan. I will guide you through some of the reasons growing numbers of people are choosing vegan meats over animal-based meats. You will also find suggestions and considerations to keep in mind when shopping for products within some of the most popular categories of vegan meats.

Why Vegan Meats?

With new and more categories of vegan meat products hitting the grocery store shelves, vegan meat has come a long way in gaining the attention of skeptics everywhere over the last few years. Gone are the days when giving up meat called for eliminating favorite meals from the dinner table. Vegan meats have gone mainstream in a big way, showing up everywhere from grocer meat cases to restaurant menus and TV commercials and challenging consumers to give meat-free meats a try. Grocery store chains such as Whole Foods, Trader Joe's, Wegmans, and Aldi, among others, are even cashing in on the demand by developing their own lines of vegan meats.

The widening accessibility of vegan meats on the market today has opened up a whole new world of options for people who are already living the vegan or vegetarian lifestyle, as well as flexitarians who enjoy experimenting with Meatless Mondays or other ways of cutting back on animal meat consumption.

With so many vegan meats so closely mimicking the texture and flavor profiles of their animal-based meat counterparts, it's only natural that people have begun to ask themselves, "When I have the option of consuming vegan meat made from plants, or meat from an animal, why do I choose one over the other?" Maybe another question consumers should be asking themselves is, "Why not vegan meats?"

It's Good for Your Health

There are massive amounts of research available online confirming the health benefits of reducing or eliminating animal-based meat from our diets, with vegan meats often cited as a healthier alternative for those who still want to enjoy the flavors they love while lowering their risk for certain ailments such as heart disease, cancers, and other health problems including diabetes, arthritis, and dementia.

Here's something to consider: The World Health Organization (WHO) officially classifies red meat as a class 2 carcinogen, which means that it "probably causes cancer" in humans. The WHO also ranks processed meat—which includes deli meats, hot dogs, and bacon—as a class 1 carcinogen alongside asbestos and cigarettes as being "known to cause cancer" in humans.

What about protein? It's a question many vegans get asked frequently. The fact is, vegan meats do contain protein. The difference between vegan meat protein and animal-derived protein is that the source of the nutrient is plant-based, usually peas or beans. Harvard University conducted a study comparing how vegan meat, specifically two popular brands of vegan ground beef, stacked up nutritionally against animal-based ground beef. What they found is that the vegan meats tested contained as much or even more protein than their meat-based counterparts.

It's Good for the Earth

Although the vegan meat market still makes up a relatively small volume of the world meat market overall, there is no question that vegan meats are far less damaging to the environment than animal-sourced meats.

As the percentage of vegan meats made continues to increase in comparison to traditional meats produced through factory farming, it is expected that we will eventually begin to see a significant decrease in worldwide greenhouse emissions, land use, and water use.

This is great news; however, legitimate climate change can come about only with considerable modifications involving our reduction or elimination of mass animal-derived meat production.

Keep in mind that every time you make the decision to purchase vegan meat over animal-based meat, you are casting a vote in favor of beneficial climate change.

Your Guide to Vegan Meats

A trip down the vegan meat aisle can feel a little daunting, especially if you are new to vegan cooking. Don't worry; I've got you covered. A little preparation goes a long way toward navigating the vegan meat section of your grocery store with confidence.

In this section, I'm going to take you through the types of vegan meats that are called for in the recipes in this book, along with the names of some of my personal favorite brands. Keep in mind that this list is not inclusive of every class of vegan meats on the market. Rather, these are general categories that I have found to be most readily available in conventional supermarkets across the United States.

// The Carbon Footprint of a Hamburger //

Did you know? Just one serving of an industrially produced animal-based burger has far-reaching effects beyond the plate.

Studies conducted by multiple universities and organizations, including Vanderbilt University, PETA (People for the Ethical Treatment of Animals), the Water Footprint Network, Greenpeace, and the U.S. Environmental Protection Agency, report staggering statistics on critical environmental issues. Global warming effects, excessive water consumption, increased pollution, and other negative environmental impacts have all been found to be directly linked to the practice of farming animals for food production.

It is estimated that the entire means of getting one ¼-pound hamburger into the hands of its end consumer—including feeding and housing a single cow, slaughtering and processing the animal for meat, then finally transporting that meat to supermarkets and restaurants—requires:

about **450** gallons of water or more	more than **½** acre of land	roughly **13** pounds of feed	and contributes to the emission **of up to 4** pounds of greenhouse gases.

Multiply those numbers by the estimated 50 billion beef burgers produced every year in the United States alone and we're talking massive amounts of natural resources being depleted around the world at an overwhelming rate every day . . . all for one hamburger.

Here's the good news: By comparison, the carbon footprint of a plant-based burger is estimated at 89 percent lower overall! The production of a vegan burger simply doesn't require the same vast amounts of land use and consumption of water resources. Choosing plant-based burgers over beef or other animal-based burgers is a simple and easy way you can make a big, good impact on the environment.

Ground "Meat"

Vegan ground meats are a total game changer. If your goal is to shift toward cooking more vegan meals, this is an excellent starting point. When you go to purchase vegan ground beef for a recipe, you will likely encounter several options from which to choose. The first thing you should know is that vegan ground beef and "veggie meat crumbles" are not the same thing.

Although both have the appearance and taste of ground beef, there are a few differences that have to do with texture and the types of recipes for which each is best suited. I personally find veggie crumbles to be the less versatile of the two, and the reason for this is simple: Veggie crumbles don't stick together. Because of the crumbly texture, they can't be shaped in the way that you would if you were making, for example, a burger. Veggie crumbles are more suited for recipes where you don't need or want that sort of shape retention, such as in soups or tacos.

Vegan ground beef is an amazing product because some brands, especially Impossible Foods and Beyond Meat, look and cook exactly like the animal-based version. This makes for an easy way to take classic ground beef–based recipes and give them new life as vegan dishes. I have done this with countless family recipes, some of which are included in this book, such as meat loaf, casseroles, roasts, and burgers, to name a few.

If you're still wondering where to use vegan ground meat, start by thinking of foods you've enjoyed in the past that have included ground meat. Then swap that animal-based meat for vegan meat and you're all set. I promise you won't miss the old version.

IMPOSSIBLE MEAT

Impossible Foods is one of the biggest players in the growing vegan meat industry today. Its Impossible ground beef and burger patties are revolutionary in that the products truly mimic the look, sounds, and flav ors of cooking meat. Impossible even fortifies its "meat" with vitamin B_{12}. The brand also adds beet juice to its product, which gives the appearance of "blood" when it's cooked. Although that may sound a bit extreme to some, especially long-term vegans, it's actually been a huge selling point with meat-eating consumers who are looking to incorporate more vegan meals into their routines. For the most realistic vegan ground meat, Impossible gets my vote.

BEYOND BEEF FROM BEYOND MEAT

Beyond Meat is a close competitor to Impossible Foods with sub-brands that currently include Beyond Beef, Beyond Sausage, and Beyond Burger. There is even some speculation that by the time this book goes to print there may be a Beyond Bacon on the market. That's how fast the vegan meat market is evolving. The quality of the brand's current offerings is outstanding for taste and texture and, like Impossible, Beyond earns bonus points for adding vitamin B_{12}, plant-based iron, and zinc to its burgers, further simulating the nutritional makeup of a beef burger.

Burgers

Vegan meat burgers are everywhere these days, from the frozen-food aisle of grocery and big-box stores to fast-food and upscale casual restaurant menus. Vegan meat patties differ from traditional "garden-style" veggie burgers that were never meant to taste like meat in that they are purposely designed to replicate the look, taste, and texture of a raw meat-based burger. Impossible and Beyond Beef are currently dominating the raw vegan meat burger sector, but others, including Trader Joe's vegan turkey burgers, are hot on their heels with their expansion beyond beef-style burgers.

Roasts

Premade vegan meat roasts have gotten a bad rap over the years and for good reason: They just weren't very good. The taste, texture, and sometimes even the presentation were missing the mark in a major way. Today, however, companies such as Field Roast and Gardein have listened to consumer feedback and adapted to meet the challenge of creating products that customers can feel confident serving for everyday dinners and special occasions, and the skyrocketing sales speak for themselves. Field Roast's Celebration Roast, Gardein's Holiday Roast, and Trader Joe's Breaded Turkey-Less Stuffed Roast are all reminiscent of a Thanksgiving turkey dinner and are huge sellers over the holiday season.

Sausages

Just as with vegan ground beef, vegan sausage is rapidly gaining popularity with vegans and nonvegans alike. It's juicy and flavorful and cooks exactly the same way as meat-based sausages. For grilling, you can't beat Beyond Meat's Italian-spiced and bratwurst Beyond Sausage links, but I'm sure some other company is trying, and I look forward to seeing what they come up with.

For most of the vegan sausage recipes in this book, I use Beyond Meat's Beyond Sausage links. There are a couple of recipes that call for Mexican chorizo–style sausage (Queso Fundido, page 12, and "Chicken" and "Chorizo" Paella, page 66); for those I like Trader Joe's Soy Chorizo, but you can also use another similar soy-based chorizo instead. No Evil Foods and MorningStar, among other brands, also make tasty vegan chorizo sausage.

Breakfast sausages are a whole other subcategory of vegan sausages. In the style of meat-based breakfast sausages, they come packaged in either links or patties. They're an easy side dish with other breakfast foods but can also be quite tasty folded into breakfast burritos or casseroles.

"Bacon"

Vegan bacon hasn't made the same great strides as other categories of vegan meats, but it's making progress in the right direction. You'll get the smoky and salty flavor you expect from bacon, but the appearance still gives it away as vegan. Of the brands widely available in the mass market today, Sweet Earth's Benevolent Bacon is my current favorite. However, with several other brands of vegan meats working to develop and improve on their own vegan bacon products, chances are there will be many more vegan bacon options on the market soon.

"Chicken"

Chicken cutlets, strips, fillets, and nuggets all have vegan doppelgangers, and they are giving the "real" thing a run for its money! The texture is chewy and can usually be shredded in a way that you would expect from meat-based chicken. I use Gardein-brand vegan chicken products most frequently, but there are lots of other good options such as No Evil Foods, Sweet Earth, and some store brands like 365 by Whole Foods.

// Food Sensitivities and Vegan Meats //

As with many types of foods, all vegan meats are not created equal and certain brands may contain ingredients that are problematic for some people, particularly those who are prone to digestive issues. Soy and gluten are commonly found in many brands of vegan meats. This doesn't mean that you are excluded from enjoying vegan meats altogether, but it does mean that you are going to have to do your homework and become a label reader.

Generally speaking, the key ingredients to look for if you have food sensitivities are soy and gluten.

Soy is the product of processed soybeans and can be used as the plant-based source of protein in vegan meats. It is a complete protein, which means that it contains all the essential amino acids our bodies need. Unfortunately, allergic reactions to soy can be quite common. The American Academy of Allergy, Asthma, and Immunology ranks soy as one of the top eight allergens in the United States, along with dairy, nuts, eggs, fish, and wheat. Which brings us to the next ingredient to watch: gluten.

Gluten is the collective name assigned to the family of proteins that are found in grains, including wheat, rye, and barley. When the gluten-containing grains are blended with water, the result is a glue-like consistency that is commonly used in foods to help them retain their shape. Many people can consume gluten without any ill side effects, but for those with issues such as celiac disease or wheat allergies, it is best to steer clear of products containing gluten.

Beyond Meat advertises that their products contain no soy and are made with gluten-free pea protein. That's great, but what is true for one brand may not be the case with another. For example, Impossible Foods is also gluten-free but their products contain soy. It's a similar situation with Gardein, which also has several gluten-free offerings such as their Beefless Ground, but many of their foods have a soy protein base. For those avoiding soy, Field Roast products and Sweet Earth burgers, among others, are good choices.

The bottom line is you are the best judge of what is right for your body, and the best way to keep yourself informed in the rapidly changing world of vegan meats is to use your best judgment and read the labels.

About the Recipes

The recipes in this book are organized by type of meal. These are conventional categories that are frequently used for cooking in general and for the dinner hour in particular. The recipes are grouped in this way to make dinner planning a snap. I know I like to mix up our weekly meals, not just with ingredients but maybe a soup one night and burgers or enchiladas the next. You can flip open a different chapter for each day and add whatever you land on to the dinner plan for the week.

All the vegan meats called for in the recipes within this book are products that I have personally found to be widely available in major supermarkets and retail stores. You will also find several recipes that call for vegan chicken-style or beef-style broth. For this, I use Better Than Bouillon's No Chicken Base and No Beef Base. Both can be found in the soup or vegan specialty aisles of major retailers.

As a heads up, many store-bought ingredients that may seem vegan at first glance may actually contain animal byproducts such as eggs, dairy, anchovies, or even animal enzymes. Always check the labels when purchasing breads, beers, and premade sauces to make sure they do not contain animal byproducts. Additionally, you may notice that many of the recipes in this book have a higher-than-average sodium count. The reason is that many of the vegan "meat" products available on the market today tend to contain high amounts of sodium—something to keep any eye out for if you're trying to limit your sodium intake.

All the recipes have been tested and given the seal of approval by my family, which is made up of vegans, vegetarians, and meat eaters. Each recipe was created with the intention of replicating favorite meals from my pre-vegan days in a way that embodies the spirit of the dish while using ingredients that are kind to animal and Earth alike.

Cocktail "Meatballs" // p. 14

Chapter 2

START ME UP

Queso Fundido

The popular restaurant appetizer of melted cheese and smoky chorizo sausage is easy to make, and the name alone is just so fun to say—say it with me: *kei-sew foon-dee-doh!* Queso fundido, which translates literally to "molten cheese," is best served in a cast-iron skillet. This helps keep the cheese hot and makes for a great presentation.

2 cups shredded vegan Cheddar cheese

2 cups shredded vegan Monterey Jack cheese

8 ounces vegan chorizo-style sausage, casings removed

1 tablespoon vegetable oil

¼ cup diced white onion

1 jalapeño pepper, finely diced

½ cup diced tomatoes

2 tablespoons chopped fresh cilantro, for garnish (optional)

Tortilla chips or warm tortillas, for serving

1. Preheat the oven to 350°F.

2. Combine the cheeses in a medium bowl, tossing to blend well.

3. Heat an 8-inch cast-iron skillet over medium-high heat. Crumble the sausage into the hot pan. Cook for 5 minutes until browned, stirring frequently to break up the meat. Remove from the heat and transfer the cooked sausage to a separate medium bowl.

4. Place the skillet back over the heat. Pour in the vegetable oil, then add the onion and jalapeño. Cook for 2 minutes, until the onions are softened. Add to the bowl with the sausage; stir to combine.

5. To assemble, spread half of the cheese in an even layer on the bottom of the skillet. Spread the sausage, pepper, and onion layer over the cheese. Top with the remaining cheese. Bake for 20 minutes, until the cheese is melted.

6. Remove from the oven and top with the diced tomatoes and cilantro (if using). Serve immediately with tortilla chips or warm tortillas.

Per Serving (without tortilla): Calories: 626; Fat: 50g; Carbohydrates: 9g; Protein: 39g; Fiber: 2g; Sodium: 923mg

"Turkey" Club Pinwheels

I really like these pinwheels because they are super simple to put together and are full of the traditional turkey club sandwich flavors we all know and love. Back in the day, a club sandwich was among my favorite things to order at the local sandwich shop, and I can still enjoy the flavor combination thanks to the variety of vegan deli meats available today. This no-cooking-required appetizer is easy to pack up and take anywhere, making it great for casual gatherings such as bridal and baby showers, backyard barbecues, and family picnics.

¼ cup vegan mayonnaise

¼ teaspoon garlic powder

¼ teaspoon onion powder

¼ teaspoon seasoned salt

¼ teaspoon freshly ground black pepper

2 burrito-size flour tortillas

1 cup shredded lettuce

16 vegan turkey-style deli slices

½ cup shredded vegan Cheddar cheese

4 slices vegan bacon, cooked and crumbled

1 Roma tomato, thinly sliced and patted dry

1. In a small bowl, stir together the vegan mayonnaise, garlic powder, onion powder, seasoned salt, and pepper until well combined.

2. Place the tortillas on a flat work surface. Divide the mayonnaise between the tortillas and spread to cover the surface of each tortilla.

3. Arrange layers of lettuce, vegan turkey, cheese, vegan bacon, and tomato over the tortillas.

4. Tightly roll each tortilla and place seam-side down. Using a serrated knife, cut the rolls into 1-inch slices and serve.

Per Serving: Calories: 166; Fat: 12g; Carbohydrates: 18g; Protein: 18g; Fiber: 1g; Sodium: 900mg

Cocktail "Meatballs"

PREP TIME: 10 minutes

COOK TIME: 1 hour
15 minutes

SERVES 6

My mother-in-law Esther's meatballs were legendary. She would bring her slow cooker full of them to every holiday celebration, where they would disappear in record time. One day she revealed to me her time-saving secret ingredient to making an already simple recipe even easier: store-bought meatballs! There are lots of varieties of vegan meatballs in the freezer section of the supermarket; look for ones that are still in their "raw meat" form and ready to cook. Make these meatballs on the stove top, or be like Esther and toss them in the slow cooker (see Cooking Variation). Either way, they'll be a hit at your next party.

24 uncooked plant-based meatballs, such as Beyond Meat meatballs

12 ounces tomato-based chili sauce

8 ounces jellied cranberry sauce

1 tablespoon brown sugar

1½ teaspoons freshly squeezed lemon juice

1. Preheat the oven to 375°F. Line a baking sheet with parchment paper.

2. Divide each meatball in half and roll into 2 mini meatballs for a total of 48 meatballs.

3. Arrange the meatballs on the prepared baking sheet so that they are at least 1 inch apart. Bake for 15 minutes, turning the meatballs once halfway through the cooking time.

4. In a medium saucepan over medium heat, stir together the chili sauce, cranberry sauce, brown sugar, and lemon juice. Cook until the sugar has dissolved, stirring frequently.

5. Turn down the heat to low and add the meatballs, stirring gently to coat with the sauce. Simmer for 1 hour before serving.

COOKING VARIATION: To make these cocktail meatballs in a slow cooker, gently toss the baked meatballs in the sauce, then place in a slow cooker on low heat for 4 hours.

Per Serving: Calories: 358; Fat: 11g; Carbohydrates: 37g; Protein: 27g; Fiber: 9g; Sodium: 920mg

Spicy "Chicken" Taquitos

PREP TIME: 15 minutes
COOK TIME: 25 minutes
SERVES 4

These rolled tacos are baked to crispy perfection and pair exceptionally well with dipping sides of freshly made guacamole, salsa, or vegan sour cream. I prefer to use corn tortillas, but if that doesn't suit your style, flour tortillas will work just as well. These taquitos also freeze beautifully.

10 ounces vegan
   chicken-style strips

2 teaspoons freshly squeezed
   lime juice

1 teaspoon chili powder

1 teaspoon ground cumin

½ teaspoon garlic powder

½ teaspoon onion powder

¼ teaspoon salt

1 cup shredded vegan
   Cheddar cheese

12 corn tortillas

Nonstick cooking spray

1. Preheat the oven to 400°F. Line a baking sheet with parchment paper.

2. Cook the vegan chicken strips according to package directions. Using two forks, pull the strips apart until they are completely shredded.

3. In a medium bowl, combine the shredded vegan chicken, lime juice, chili powder, ground cumin, garlic powder, onion powder, and salt. Toss to coat the "chicken" shreds in the spices. Add the cheese and toss again to combine.

4. Wrap the tortillas in a damp paper towel and microwave for 1 minute. This will soften the tortillas and make them more flexible for rolling. Keep the tortillas covered so that they stay warm, removing only one at a time.

5. To assemble the taquitos, lay the tortillas on a flat work surface. Onto each warm tortilla, add 2 tablespoons of filling. Fold one side over the filling, tucking it in tightly. Continue rolling up the taquito and place seam-side down on the prepared baking sheet. Continue with the remaining tortillas and filling.

6. Spray the taquitos generously with cooking spray. Bake for 20 minutes, until crispy and golden brown, then serve.

Per Serving: Calories: 473; Fat: 19g; Carbohydrates: 47g; Protein: 31g; Fiber: 7g; Sodium: 1,134mg

Beer-Glazed "Bratwurst" Bites

PREP TIME: 5 minutes

COOK TIME: 30 minutes

SERVES 6

No big game party or tailgating event is complete without the distinctive and "meaty" pairing of sausage and beer, and this vegan version scores major flavor points. Since it is mild enough to avoid overpowering the flavor of the sausages, a smooth lager brew is a good choice here. As lighter beers cook down, they leave behind a nice, syrupy-sweet flavor, whereas darker beers tend to impart a more intense beer flavor.

8 vegan bratwurst-style sausage links

12 ounces lager-style beer

½ cup brown sugar

1 tablespoon creamy Dijon mustard

⅛ teaspoon freshly ground black pepper

2 teaspoons cornstarch

1 tablespoon water

1. Cook the sausage links according to the package directions, then slice them into pieces 1 inch thick. Set aside.

2. While the sausages are cooking, set a medium saucepan over medium-high heat. In the saucepan, gently stir together the beer and brown sugar. Bring to a boil for 1 minute, dissolving the sugar, then turn down the heat to low. Simmer for 20 minutes, until the sauce reduces to about half its original volume. Stir in the mustard and season with black pepper.

3. In a small bowl, whisk together the cornstarch and water to make a slurry, then pour the slurry into the sauce. Continue cooking and stirring frequently for 5 minutes, until the sauce is thickened.

4. Add the sausage slices and stir to thoroughly coat with the sauce before serving.

COOKING TIP: Use a slow cooker on the lowest setting to keep the sausage bites warm for grazing guests. Keep it casual with colorful plates and festive toothpicks for serving.

Per Serving: Calories: 185; Fat: 6g; Carbohydrates: 24g; Protein: 7g; Fiber: 1g; Sodium: 332mg

Blackened "Steak" Bites

Tender beef-style tips smothered in a bold mix of spices and then pan-seared and dipped in garlic butter sauce are one of the easiest appetizers you'll ever make. The seasoning has a kick to it. To reduce the heat, you can leave out the cayenne.

1 teaspoon dried thyme

¾ teaspoon paprika

2½ teaspoons garlic powder, divided

½ teaspoon onion powder

½ teaspoon freshly ground black pepper

1 teaspoon salt, divided

¼ teaspoon dried oregano

¼ teaspoon cayenne pepper

⅛ teaspoon ground cumin

2 (9-ounce) packages meatless beef tips, such as Gardein Home Style Beefless Tips

1 tablespoon vegetable oil

8 tablespoons (1 stick) vegan butter, divided

2 tablespoons minced garlic

1 tablespoon finely chopped fresh parsley

1. In a small bowl, combine the thyme, paprika, ½ teaspoon of garlic powder, onion powder, black pepper, ½ teaspoon of salt, oregano, cayenne pepper, and cumin. Set aside.

2. Place the "beef" tips in a medium bowl and sprinkle with the seasoning. Toss to coat.

3. In a large skillet over medium-high heat, heat the vegetable oil. When the oil is hot, add the seasoned "beef" tips. Cook for 5 minutes, turning occasionally, until lightly seared on all sides (work in batches, if necessary, to avoid crowding the pan). Set aside.

4. Put 2 tablespoons of butter into a small saucepan over medium heat. When the butter is melted, add the garlic. Cook for 1 minute, stirring constantly.

5. Add the remaining 6 tablespoons of butter, remaining 2 teaspoons of garlic powder, and remaining ½ teaspoon of salt. Continue cooking, stirring occasionally, until all the butter is melted.

6. Remove from the heat and stir in the parsley. Pour the garlic butter into a serving dish and serve alongside the "steak" bites.

Per Serving: Calories: 464; Fat: 35g; Carbohydrates: 14g; Protein: 22g; Fiber: 1g; Sodium: 1,314mg

Lumpia Shanghai

Making these small but mighty Filipino-style spring rolls is a labor of love, for sure. With one crunchy bite, though, I promise your efforts will be rewarded. Because of the time involved, you may want to make a big batch and freeze some for an easy, anytime appetizer or snack.

10 ounces vegan pork shreds (discard the sauce packet, if included)

1 cup very thinly sliced green cabbage

½ cup shredded carrot

¼ cup finely diced yellow onion

2 garlic cloves, minced

½ teaspoon salt

¼ teaspoon freshly ground black pepper

12 spring roll wrappers

2 cups vegetable oil, or as needed, for frying

½ cup sweet chili sauce, for dipping

1. Cook the vegan pork shreds according to the package directions.

2. In a large bowl, stir together the vegan pork, cabbage, carrot, onion, garlic, salt, and black pepper.

3. Place a small bowl of water nearby and assemble the lumpia shanghai by placing wrappers one at a time onto a flat work surface with a corner of the wrapper pointing toward you.

4. Put 1 heaping tablespoon of filling on the bottom third of the wrapper and use your hands to shape the filling into a narrow log shape horizontally across the wrapper. Roll the bottom corner of the wrapper up and over the filling, tucking the corner snugly under the filling. Tuck the left and right corners over the sides and continue rolling the rest of the way. Dip your fingers into the water and run them along the edge to seal the wrapper. Repeat with the remaining wrappers and filling.

5. In a large, deep skillet over medium-high heat, heat the vegetable oil. The exact amount of oil needed will depend on the size of your pan and should be enough to cover the lumpia at least halfway; adjust the amount of oil you use accordingly. Line a plate with paper towels.

6. When the oil is hot, add a few lumpia. Cook for 3 minutes, turning halfway through, until golden brown.

7. Remove from the heat and transfer the cooked lumpia to the prepared plate to drain the excess oil.

8. Serve hot with sweet chili sauce for dipping.

COOKING TIP: Lumpia is best cooked in batches to avoid overcrowding the pan, which can lead to lowering the temperature of the cooking oil.

Per Serving: Calories: 611; Fat: 24g; Carbohydrates: 69g; Protein: 28g; Fiber: 7g; Sodium: 1,813mg

PREP TIME: 10 minutes

COOK TIME: 20 minutes

SERVES 6

"Sausage"-Stuffed Mini Peppers

I've always loved seeing the big bags of colorful mini peppers at the supermarket, but for the longest time I had no idea what in the world to do with them. Turns out, they're perfect for stuffing. They're like little red and yellow and orange boats delivering creamy and savory sausage directly to your mouth. Yum. These stuffed peppers are right at home everywhere from a laid-back brunch to a swanky dinner party.

½ pound mini sweet peppers, halved lengthwise

4 ounces vegan Italian-style sausage

4 ounces vegan cream cheese

¼ cup shredded vegan Cheddar cheese

1 tablespoon Italian-seasoned bread crumbs

1 tablespoon chopped fresh chives

1 teaspoon minced garlic

¼ teaspoon freshly ground black pepper

1. Preheat the oven to 350°F.

2. Arrange the sweet pepper halves in an even layer on a baking sheet.

3. Crumble the sausage into a medium skillet over medium heat. Cook for 5 minutes until heated through, stirring frequently to break up the sausage.

4. Transfer the cooked sausage to a medium bowl. Add the cream cheese, Cheddar cheese, bread crumbs, chives, garlic, and black pepper. Stir to evenly distribute the ingredients.

5. Fill each sweet pepper half with a heaping spoonful of the sausage and cheese mixture.

6. Bake for 15 minutes. Switch the oven's heat setting to a high broil. Broil the peppers for 1 minute, just enough to lightly crisp the tops of the filling, then serve.

Per Serving: Calories: 138; Fat: 10g; Carbohydrates: 6g; Protein: 7g; Fiber: 1g; Sodium: 377mg

White "Chicken" Chili // p. 30

Chapter 3

SENSATIONAL SOUPS, STEWS, AND CHILIS

"Chicken" Noodle Soup

PREP TIME: 10 minutes

COOK TIME: 30 minutes

SERVES 4 TO 6

This recipe takes me back to sick days in the '80s. It was all about lounging on the couch completely captivated by the latest music videos on MTV and the game show theater of *The Price Is Right*. And when lunchtime rolled around, chicken soup was the special of the day. When you're under the weather or just want a big hot bowl of comfort on a chilly day, wrap yourself in a blanket and cozy up with a good old-fashioned bowl of vegan chicken noodle soup. Don't forget the sleeve of saltine crackers on the side.

8 ounces medium spiral pasta

3 tablespoons vegan butter, divided

10 ounces vegan chicken-style strips

1 cup sliced baby carrots

1 cup diced celery

1 cup diced yellow onion

8 cups vegan chicken-style broth

2 teaspoons poultry seasoning

½ teaspoon dried basil

½ teaspoon dried oregano

1. Cook the noodles according to the package directions for al dente consistency. Drain and rinse with cold water to stop the cooking process. Set aside.

2. In a large soup pot over medium-high heat, heat 1 tablespoon of butter. When the butter is melted, add the vegan chicken strips. Cook for 5 minutes to brown on both sides. Transfer the cooked strips to a cutting board and roughly chop.

3. Add the remaining 2 tablespoons of butter to the pot. When the butter is melted, add the carrots, celery, and onion. Cook for 3 minutes, stirring frequently, until slightly crisp-tender.

4. Stir in the chopped vegan chicken, broth, poultry seasoning, basil, and oregano. Bring to a boil, then turn down the heat to low. Cover the pot and simmer for 20 minutes.

5. Stir in the cooked noodles and serve.

Per Serving: Calories: 480; Fat: 19g; Carbohydrates: 53g; Protein: 25g; Fiber: 7g; Sodium: 618mg

Lasagna Soup

This is a fun way to enjoy the flavors of a good old-fashioned Italian-style lasagna casserole in an easy-to-make soup. What makes this delicious soup especially interesting is watching how other people choose to eat it. Although it is technically a soup, you might need a fork *and* a spoon. A fork for the lasagna noodles and a spoon for the . . . well, for the soup. *Buon appetito!*

14 ounces vegan sweet Italian-style sausage

6 ounces vegan ground beef

½ cup diced yellow onion

1 tablespoon minced garlic

1 (28-ounce) can crushed tomatoes

4 cups vegan beef-style broth

8 ounces tomato sauce

1½ teaspoons Italian seasoning

10 lasagna noodles, broken into pieces

½ cup shredded vegan mozzarella cheese, for garnish (optional)

½ cup shredded vegan Parmesan cheese, for garnish (optional)

2 tablespoons chopped fresh flat-leaf parsley, for garnish (optional)

1. Into a large soup pot over medium-high heat, crumble the sausage and vegan ground beef. Use a spatula to break up any large pieces. Add the onion and cook for 6 minutes, stirring frequently, until browned. Add the garlic and continue cooking for 1 minute more.

2. Add the tomatoes, broth, tomato sauce, and Italian seasoning. Bring to a boil, then add the lasagna noodle pieces. Turn down the heat to low. Cover and simmer for 20 minutes, until the noodles are softened.

3. Ladle into soup bowls. Garnish with mozzarella, Parmesan, and parsley (if using), then serve.

Per Serving: Calories: 614; Fat: 21g; Carbohydrates: 76g; Protein: 39g; Fiber: 12g; Sodium: 1,441mg

PREP TIME: 10 minutes

COOK TIME: 35 minutes

SERVES 4 TO 6

Black-Eyed Pea and "Bratwurst" Stew

Confession: I used to eat black-eyed peas only one day out of the entire year and that day was January 1. I don't know why it never occurred to me to have them any other time; it's not like beans are a seasonal item. Turns out, black-eyed peas are not just for New Year's Day after all, my friends. This soup actually puts me in mind of Oktoberfest season. It's warm and hearty with beans, vegan bratwurst, and potatoes. Plus, the addition of Buffalo-style wing sauce gives a nice and spicy kick.

28 ounces vegan bratwurst-style sausage links, cut into 1-inch pieces

½ cup diced yellow onion

4 cups vegan chicken-style broth

2 (15-ounce) cans black-eyed peas, drained and rinsed

1½ cups cubed potatoes (½-inch cubes)

1½ cups trimmed green beans (2-inch pieces)

1½ tablespoons vegan Worcestershire sauce

1 tablespoon Buffalo-style wing sauce

1 tablespoon tomato-based ketchup

1 teaspoon minced garlic

¼ teaspoon dried thyme

¼ cup all-purpose flour

2 tablespoons water

1. In a large soup pot over medium-high heat, cook the sausage and onion for 5 minutes, turning frequently, until the sausages are browned.

2. Stir in the broth, black-eyed peas, potatoes, green beans, Worcestershire, Buffalo sauce, ketchup, garlic, and thyme.

3. Bring to a boil, then turn down the heat to low. Simmer for 20 minutes, until the potatoes are fork-tender.

4. In a small bowl, whisk together the flour and water, making a slurry. Stir the slurry into the stew and continue simmering for 10 minutes more to thicken the soup slightly.

5. Ladle into soup bowls and serve.

Per Serving: Calories: 799; Fat: 37g; Carbohydrates: 78g; Protein: 51g; Fiber: 20g; Sodium: 1,718mg

"Pork" and Vegetable Stew

This is a thick and chunky stew that is packed with colorful vegetables and rich with flavor. Vegan pork bites add a depth of flavor that takes this from an ordinary vegetable soup to an extraordinary stew that is sure to become a new cool-weather favorite. I like to pair this nourishing stew with a simple side of warm, crusty bread.

20 ounces vegan pork bites

2 tablespoons all-purpose flour

1 teaspoon salt, divided

½ teaspoon freshly ground
   black pepper

2 tablespoons vegan butter

½ cup diced yellow onion

½ cup sliced celery

1 cup sliced carrots

4 cups vegan chicken-style
   broth or vegetable broth

14 ounces stewed tomatoes
   with garlic, herbs, and onions

2 cups cubed baby red potatoes
   (1-inch cubes)

1 teaspoon dried oregano

1 bay leaf

1 cup trimmed green beans
   (2-inch pieces)

½ cup frozen corn kernels

Fresh flat-leaf parsley, chopped,
   for garnish (optional)

1. In a large bowl, combine the vegan pork bites, flour, ½ teaspoon of salt, and black pepper. Toss to coat.

2. In a large soup pot over medium-high heat, heat the butter. When the butter is melted, add the seasoned pork bites, onion, celery, and carrots. Cook for 5 minutes, turning frequently, until browned on all sides.

3. Add the remaining ½ teaspoon of salt, broth, tomatoes, potatoes, oregano, and bay leaf. Bring to a boil, then turn down the heat to low.

4. Simmer for 20 minutes, until the potatoes are fork-tender. Stir in the green beans and corn, then continue simmering for 10 minutes more. Remove and discard the bay leaf.

5. Ladle into soup bowls, then garnish with parsley (if using) and serve.

INGREDIENT TIP: If stewed tomatoes are too much . . . tomato . . . in one bite for your taste, they can easily be swapped out for diced tomatoes without affecting the outcome of the stew.

Per Serving: Calories: 503; Fat: 24g; Carbohydrates: 35g; Protein: 37g; Fiber: 9g; Sodium: 1,978mg

"Beef" and Rice Stew

PREP TIME: 20 minutes
COOK TIME: 30 minutes
SERVES 4

There is just something about this stew that makes it one of my favorites during the gradual transition to cooler weather. This recipe forms a great base that offers a lot of flexibility. Sometimes I mix up the vegetables depending on what I have handy that day. Potatoes, carrots, celery, and corn are all good additions or substitutions. Play around with the recipe and find your favorite version.

2 tablespoons vegetable oil

18 ounces vegan beef tips

½ teaspoon garlic powder

1 teaspoon salt, divided

1 teaspoon freshly ground black pepper, divided

1 cup stemmed and sliced cremini mushrooms

1 cup diced green bell pepper

½ cup diced yellow onion

6 cups vegan beef-style broth

¼ cup red wine

¼ cup tomato paste

1 bay leaf

2 cups cooked long-grain white rice

Fresh flat-leaf parsley, chopped, for garnish (optional)

1. In a large skillet over medium-high heat, heat the vegetable oil. When the oil is hot, add the vegan beef tips. Season with the garlic powder, ½ teaspoon of salt, and ½ teaspoon of black pepper. Cook for 5 minutes, turning frequently, until browned on all sides. Set aside.

2. In a large soup pot over medium-high heat, combine the mushrooms, bell pepper, and onion. Cook for 3 minutes, stirring frequently, until softened.

3. Stir in the broth, wine, tomato paste, the remaining ½ teaspoon of salt, the remaining ½ teaspoon of pepper, and the bay leaf. Bring to a boil, then turn down the heat to low.

4. Cover and simmer for 15 minutes. Add the vegan beef tips and cooked rice, then continue simmering for 5 minutes more.

5. Ladle into bowls, garnish with parsley (if using), and serve.

INGREDIENT TIP: Note that this recipe calls for rice that is already cooked. Pre-cooking the rice ensures that it doesn't get overcooked and also serves to help thicken the stew with its natural starches.

Per Serving: Calories: 487; Fat: 19g; Carbohydrates: 43g; Protein: 32g; Fiber: 2g; Sodium: 1,294mg

Italian Chili

Any dish that includes pasta immediately gets my attention. Generally speaking, pasta is not widely considered a common ingredient in chili; however, this is where we throw convention out the window. In addition to pasta, this recipe uses vegan ground beef to give you that classic chili texture and flavor.

14 ounces vegan ground beef

¼ cup olive oil

1½ cups chopped yellow onion

1 cup chopped celery

¼ cup minced garlic

½ teaspoon freshly ground black pepper

4 cups vegan beef-style broth or vegetable broth

14 ounces diced tomatoes with Italian seasonings, drained

¼ cup chopped fresh flat-leaf parsley

3 ounces tomato paste

1¼ teaspoons dried thyme

1¼ teaspoons dried basil

1¼ teaspoons dried oregano

1 cup ditalini pasta or other small soup pasta

1 (15-ounce) can cannellini beans, drained and rinsed

1. Into a large pot over medium-high heat, crumble the vegan ground beef. Cook for 5 minutes, stirring frequently, until browned. Transfer to a bowl and set aside.

2. In the same pot, heat the olive oil. When the oil is hot, add the onion, celery, garlic, and black pepper. Cook, stirring frequently, for 3 minutes, until the vegetables are crisp-tender.

3. Stir in the broth, tomatoes, parsley, and tomato paste. Season with the thyme, basil, and oregano. Bring to a boil, then turn down the heat to low. Cover and simmer for 1 hour, stirring occasionally.

4. While the chili is simmering, cook the pasta according to the package directions. Drain and set aside.

5. Add the cooked vegan ground beef and cannellini beans to the pot with the chili. Continue simmering for an additional 10 minutes. Stir in the pasta and serve.

Per Serving: Calories: 466; Fat: 17g; Carbohydrates: 53g; Protein: 29g; Fiber: 17g; Sodium: 405mg

White "Chicken" Chili

PREP TIME: 10 minutes

COOK TIME: 1 hour
40 minutes

SERVES 4

This chili is fantastic on a cold winter day or night (but that's not to say you can't enjoy it year-round!). I love the way the herbs and seasonings fill the air with their savory aroma that wafts through the kitchen as the chili is simmering away on the stove. While this recipe does call for a decent amount of ingredients, a majority of the items are common and may likely already be in your kitchen pantry.

2 tablespoons olive oil, divided

10 ounces vegan chicken-style strips

¾ cup chopped yellow onion

8 ounces green chiles, drained and diced

½ teaspoon freshly ground black pepper

2 tablespoons minced garlic

1 (15-ounce) can cannellini beans, rinsed and drained

1 (15-ounce) can great northern beans, rinsed and drained

1 (15-ounce) can light pinto beans, rinsed and drained

2 bell peppers (1 green, 1 red), seeded and chopped

¾ cup roughly chopped fresh flat-leaf parsley

¼ cup chopped scallions

3½ cups vegan chicken-style broth

1 cup dry white wine

1½ tablespoons ground cumin

1 tablespoon dried oregano

2 teaspoons poultry seasoning

1 teaspoon dried rosemary

1 teaspoon dried thyme

2 bay leaves

Shredded vegan Cheddar cheese, for serving (optional)

1. In a large pot over medium-high heat, heat 1 tablespoon of olive oil. When the oil is hot, add the vegan chicken strips. Cook for 5 minutes, turning frequently until browned. Transfer to a cutting board and cut into ½-inch pieces.

2. To the pot, add the remaining 1 tablespoon of olive oil, the onion, green chiles, and black pepper. Cook, stirring frequently, for 1 minute, to soften the onions, then add the garlic. Continue cooking for 1 minute more.

3. Stir in the cannellini, great northern, and pinto beans, bell peppers, parsley, and scallions. Cook, stirring frequently, for 2 minutes.

4. Add the broth, wine, cumin, oregano, poultry seasoning, rosemary, thyme, and bay leaves. Bring to a boil, then turn down the heat to low. Simmer, stirring occasionally, for 90 minutes. Discard the bay leaves and stir in the cooked vegan chicken.

5. Ladle into soup bowls, then garnish with the vegan Cheddar cheese, if desired, and serve.

INGREDIENT TIP: Any of the beans listed in this recipe can be substituted with another variety, as needed. The varying shades of the three types of beans together does add to the presentation, but you can absolutely use 3 cans of the same type of bean and the chili will still be delicious.

Per Serving: Calories: 550; Fat: 18g; Carbohydrates: 57g; Protein: 34g; Fiber: 16g; Sodium: 612mg

4-Alarm Chili

PREP TIME: 10 minutes

COOK TIME: 40 minutes

SERVES 4 TO 6

I read recently that the number of "alarms" assigned to a chili recipe actually has very little to do with the amount of heat but rather is an indication of the number of pepper varieties in the pot. This recipe includes four kinds of peppers, all with distinct flavor profiles. You can dial the heat up or down by adding more or fewer to suit your preference.

- 24 ounces vegan ground beef
- 1 cup seeded and chopped Anaheim pepper
- 1 cup seeded and chopped poblano pepper
- 1 tablespoon seeded and chopped jalapeño pepper
- ½ cup diced yellow onion
- 1 tablespoon minced garlic
- 1 tablespoon chili powder
- 1 tablespoon ground cumin
- 1½ teaspoons salt
- ½ teaspoon ground coriander
- ½ teaspoon dried oregano
- ½ teaspoon freshly ground black pepper
- 2 tablespoons tomato paste
- 12 ounces lager beer
- 1 (28-ounce) can petite diced tomatoes, with their juices
- 1 (15-ounce) can pinto beans, drained and rinsed
- 1 (15-ounce) can kidney beans, drained and rinsed
- 2 tablespoons pureed chipotle peppers in adobo sauce

1. In a large pot, combine the vegan ground beef; Anaheim, poblano, and jalapeño peppers; and onion. Cook for 5 minutes, stirring frequently, until the beef is browned. Add the garlic and continue cooking for 1 minute more.

2. Add the chili powder, cumin, salt, coriander, oregano, and black pepper. Cook for 2 minutes, then add the tomato paste and cook for 2 minutes more, stirring frequently.

3. Pour in the beer and bring to a boil for 5 minutes, until the liquid is mostly cooked off.

4. Stir in the diced tomatoes with their juices, pinto beans, kidney beans, and pureed chipotle peppers. Turn down the heat to low.

5. Partially cover the pot and simmer for 30 minutes, stirring occasionally.

6. Ladle into bowls and serve. Add your favorite chili toppings, if desired.

Per Serving: Calories: 526; Fat: 6g; Carbohydrates: 65g; Protein: 51g; Fiber: 21g; Sodium: 1,830mg

Green Chile
Cheeseburgers // p. 45

Chapter 4

BURGER LOVE

"Beef" and Sausage Burgers

PREP TIME: 10 minutes
COOK TIME: 20 minutes
SERVES 6

This combination of vegan sausage and ground "beef" topped with fresh veggies and cheese will wow even the most skeptical meat eaters. The first time I served these burgers was to a group of hard-core carnivores—and they devoured them!

1 tablespoon olive oil

½ cup thinly sliced red onion

1 large green bell pepper, seeded and thinly sliced

½ pound cremini mushrooms, stemmed and thinly sliced

Salt

Freshly ground black pepper

14 ounces vegan hot Italian-style sausage links

12 ounces vegan ground beef

1 tablespoon steak seasoning spice blend

⅔ teaspoon garlic powder

¼ cup finely chopped flat-leaf parsley

6 slices vegan provolone cheese

6 pretzel burger buns

6 butter lettuce leaves

1. Heat the olive oil in a medium skillet over medium-high heat. Pour in the red onion, bell pepper, and cremini mushrooms. Cook, stirring frequently, until tender, 3 to 4 minutes, then season to taste with salt and black pepper. Set aside.

2. To make the burgers, crumble the sausage and vegan ground beef into a medium bowl. Mix in the steak seasoning spice blend, garlic powder, and parsley until thoroughly combined. Divide the burger mixture into six equal portions. Roll each portion into a ball, then use the palm of your hand to flatten each ball into a ½-inch-thick patty.

3. Heat a large cast-iron skillet or grill pan over medium-high heat. If using an outdoor grill, preheat it to 375°F. Place the patties in the preheated pan or on the direct heat side of the grill, and cook for 7 to 8 minutes per side.

4. During the last 2 minutes of cooking, top each patty with a spoonful of bell pepper and mushroom mixture, then place a slice of cheese over each. Using a lid, cover the burgers to help melt the cheese.

5. Build burgers by layering the bun bottoms, lettuce, burgers, and bun tops.

Per Serving: Calories: 497; Fat: 21g; Carbohydrates: 43g; Protein: 40g; Fiber: 9g; Sodium: 1,471mg

Sloppy Joes

I've been making these sloppy joes for years. They're always a hit with adults and kids alike. Once the vegan meat is finished simmering in the sauce, I like to leave it in the pan on the stove and serve it up family-style, allowing everyone to build their own sandwich. I've never had leftovers and you won't, either.

1 tablespoon olive oil

16 ounces vegan ground beef

¼ cup chopped yellow onion

¼ cup chopped green
bell pepper

¼ cup tomato-based ketchup

1 tablespoon brown sugar

1 teaspoon yellow mustard

½ teaspoon garlic powder

Salt

Freshly ground black pepper

4 vegan hamburger buns

1. Heat the olive oil in a medium skillet over medium heat. When the oil is hot, crumble the vegan ground beef into the pan. Add the onion and bell pepper and cook for 5 minutes, until the meat has browned and the peppers are softened.

2. Stir in the ketchup, brown sugar, yellow mustard, and garlic powder and season with salt and black pepper. Turn down the heat to low and simmer for 30 minutes.

3. Pile the sloppy joe filling onto toasted burger buns and serve.

INGREDIENT TIP: Want to crank up the heat? Add a few pickled jalapeño slices over the Sloppy Joe filling for a spicy kick in every bite!

Per Serving: Calories: 373; Fat: 8g; Carbohydrates: 48g; Protein: 26g; Fiber: 7g; Sodium: 1,073mg

Cajun-Spiced Sliders

PREP TIME: 10 minutes

COOK TIME: 15 minutes

SERVES 4

These sliders bring New Orleans flair to burger night at home. Cajun spices and the holy trinity of Cajun-style cooking—onions, bell peppers, and celery—are topped off with a homemade remoulade sauce that will have you saying, "*Laissez les bons temps rouler!*"

½ cup vegan mayonnaise

1 tablespoon Creole mustard

1½ teaspoons Louisiana-style hot pepper sauce

1 tablespoon finely chopped celery

1 tablespoon finely chopped fresh flat-leaf parsley

1 teaspoon capers, chopped

½ teaspoon salt

½ teaspoon freshly ground black pepper

24 ounces vegan ground beef

⅓ cup finely chopped scallions

2 tablespoons Cajun seasoning blend

1 tablespoon vegetable oil

1 small yellow onion, thinly sliced

1 medium green bell pepper, seeded and thinly sliced

12 vegan slider buns, lightly toasted

1. In a small bowl, stir together the mayonnaise, mustard, hot sauce, celery, parsley, capers, salt, and black pepper to create a remoulade sauce. Refrigerate until ready to use.

2. In a large bowl, crumble the vegan ground beef, then stir in the scallions and Cajun seasoning blend.

3. Divide the mixture into 12 equal portions. Roll each portion into a ball, then flatten with the palm of your hand to form patties at your desired level of thickness.

4. Heat a large cast-iron skillet or grill pan over medium-high heat. If using an outdoor grill, preheat it to 375°F. Place the patties in the preheated pan or on the direct heat side of the grill, and cook for about 4 minutes per side, or until done.

5. Heat the vegetable oil in a medium skillet over medium-high heat. Add the onion and bell pepper slices. Cook for 5 minutes, until softened and lightly charred. Season to taste with salt and pepper, then remove from the heat.

6. To assemble, lay a burger patty on each slider bun bottom. Top with remoulade sauce, bell peppers, and onions, cover with the slider bun tops, then serve.

INGREDIENT TIP: If Creole mustard is not available, whole-grain Dijon mustard will work in a pinch.

Per Serving: Calories: 616; Fat: 23g; Carbohydrates: 58g; Protein: 46g; Fiber: 15g; Sodium: 1,758mg

Crispy Fried "Chicken" Burgers

When I was a kid and my family would make fried chicken, the thick layer of golden fried breading was always my favorite part. I like these burgers for the same crunch that comes with the seasoned fried batter, and the jalapeño-ranch slaw, with its spicy coolness contrasting with the hot "chicken," just puts it over the top.

Fun fact: The secret ingredient to getting the batter to fry up extra crispy is . . . drumroll, please . . . baking powder! Something scientific and magical happens when baking powder hits the hot oil and causes the batter to get extra airy and bubbly, thereby making it less doughy and more of what we want: crispy.

½ cup vegan mayonnaise, plus more for serving

3 tablespoons Louisiana-style hot pepper sauce, divided

1 teaspoon minced garlic

4 cups thinly sliced cabbage

¼ cup thinly sliced red onion

1 jalapeño pepper, thinly sliced

2 cups all-purpose flour

1 teaspoon baking powder

1 teaspoon onion powder

1 teaspoon garlic powder

1 teaspoon cayenne pepper

1 teaspoon salt

1 teaspoon freshly ground black pepper

1 cup unsweetened plant-based milk (such as oat, cashew, or almond)

4 meatless chicken-style patties, breaded

Vegetable oil, for frying

4 vegan hamburger buns

1. In a small mixing bowl, combine the mayonnaise, 1 tablespoon of hot pepper sauce, and garlic. Add the cabbage, red onion, and jalapeño pepper. Toss to coat thoroughly, then refrigerate the slaw until ready to use.

2. Set up your dredging station: In a medium bowl, combine the flour, baking powder, onion powder, garlic powder, cayenne pepper, salt, and black pepper. Set aside. In a separate medium bowl, stir together the milk and the remaining 2 tablespoons of hot pepper sauce.

3. One at a time, submerge each chicken-style patty into the milk, then immediately press into the flour mixture, turning to coat completely. Gently shake off excess flour and dip the patty again in the milk, then again in the flour.

4. Into a large, deep skillet over medium-high heat, pour the vegetable oil. Make sure you add enough oil to submerge the patties halfway. Line a plate with paper towels.

5. When the oil is hot, gently place the coated patties in the pan. Cook for 3 minutes on each side, until fully golden and crisp. Place the cooked burgers on the prepared plate to drain excess oil.

6. Build the burgers by layering the bottom buns with mayonnaise, crispy "chicken" patties, and jalapeño ranch slaw, cover with the bun tops, then serve.

Per Serving: Calories: 600; Fat: 27g; Carbohydrates: 67g; Protein: 24g; Fiber: 7g; Sodium: 1,131mg

PREP TIME: 10 minutes

COOK TIME: 35 minutes

SERVES 4

"Bacon" and Beer Cheeseburgers

When I was a teenager, I loved going to Charlie's Hamburger Joint in Houston, Texas. Those guys made the best bacon cheeseburgers around, piled high with toppings, oozing with condiments, and already falling over before you even took the first bite. You definitely needed silverware and a stack of napkins at the ready. These saucy burgers remind me of Charlie's. You might want to have a knife and fork nearby because these burgers are messy!

2 tablespoons vegan butter

3 tablespoons all-purpose flour

½ cup mild-flavored plant-based milk (such as oat or unsweetened almond)

⅓ cup pale ale beer

1 teaspoon plus 2 tablespoons vegan Worcestershire sauce, divided

½ teaspoon creamy Dijon mustard

¼ teaspoon plus ⅛ teaspoon salt

⅛ teaspoon cayenne pepper

1 cup shredded vegan Cheddar cheese

8 slices vegan bacon

24 ounces vegan ground beef

¼ teaspoon freshly ground black pepper

4 pretzel burger buns, lightly toasted

1. Melt the butter in a medium saucepan over medium heat. Whisk in the flour; the mixture will be thick. Gradually pour in the milk, whisking constantly to incorporate. Stir in the beer, 1 teaspoon of vegan Worcestershire, the mustard, ¼ teaspoon of salt, the cayenne pepper, and the cheese. Cook for about 15 minutes, stirring frequently, until the cheese is completely melted.

2. While the sauce is cooking, cook the vegan bacon according to the package directions and set aside.

3. In a medium bowl, combine the vegan ground beef, remaining 2 tablespoons of Worcestershire, remaining ⅛ teaspoon of salt, and black pepper. Divide the mixture into four portions, then roll into balls and shape into patties.

4. Heat a large skillet or grill pan over medium-high heat. Add the burgers and cook for 4 minutes per side or until done.

5. To build the burgers, stack a patty onto each of the bottom bun slices. Top with 2 slices of bacon, smother with cheese sauce, then add a bun top and dig in!

Per Serving: Calories: 619; Fat: 22g; Carbohydrates: 52g; Protein: 52g; Fiber: 12g; Sodium: 2,220mg

Patty Melts

Patty melts always remind me of late-night diner food. The first time I ever had one was at the Tick Tock Diner in New York City after a long night on the town. That was a lifetime ago, but I still remember the night I fell in love with the patty melt. This sandwich is "beefy" and juicy, with caramelized onions giving just a hint of sweetness. Serving it on grilled rye or sourdough bread gives a satisfying crunch in every bite.

8 tablespoons (1 stick) vegan butter, divided

1 medium yellow onion, very thinly sliced

24 ounces vegan ground beef

½ teaspoon garlic powder

½ teaspoon onion powder

¾ teaspoon vegan Worcestershire sauce

¼ teaspoon salt

¼ teaspoon freshly ground black pepper

8 slices rye or sourdough bread

8 slices vegan provolone cheese

1. Line a plate with paper towels.

2. Melt 2 tablespoons of butter in a large skillet over low heat. Add the onion slices, turning them over to coat in the butter, then cook for 10 minutes or until the onion slices are caramelized. Transfer to the prepared plate and set aside. Keep the skillet out.

3. In a medium bowl, combine the vegan ground beef, garlic powder, onion powder, vegan Worcestershire sauce, salt, and black pepper. Divide the mixture into four equal portions. Roll each into a ball then shape into four patties to fit your bread.

4. Melt 2 tablespoons of butter in the skillet over medium heat. Add the patties and cook for 4 minutes on each side or until done. Remove the patties and wipe out the skillet.

5. Spread the remaining butter over one side of each slice of bread and place the bread butter-side down in the skillet still over medium heat. Next, add 1 slice of cheese, a burger patty, some caramelized onions, a second slice of cheese, and the top piece of bread, butter-side up. Cook for 4 minutes per side or until the bread is golden-crisp and the cheese is melted. Slice in half to serve.

Per Serving: Calories: 698; Fat 32g; Carbohydrates: 54g; Protein: 49g; Fiber: 14g; Sodium: 1,743mg

Green Chile Cheeseburgers

The Hatch Valley region of New Mexico is to chile peppers what Napa Valley is to American wines. The varieties range from mild to jalapeño-hot and have a short growing season of August to September. However, canned varieties are typically available year-round and are a fine substitution to use in this recipe.

4 Hatch green chiles

24 ounces vegan ground beef

1 teaspoon dried oregano

¼ teaspoon garlic powder

¼ teaspoon ground cumin

¼ teaspoon freshly ground black pepper

⅛ teaspoon salt

4 slices vegan Cheddar cheese

4 vegan hamburger buns

Creamy Dijon mustard, for serving

1. Set the oven to broil. Arrange the chiles in a roasting pan, then set under the broiler for about 10 minutes, until blackened in places. Place the roasted chiles in a plastic or paper bag to steam for 20 minutes. Remove the chiles from the bag. Rub off the blackened skins, then remove the stems and seeds. Finely chop the chiles and set aside.

2. In a medium bowl, mix together the vegan ground beef, oregano, garlic powder, cumin, black pepper, and salt. Divide the mixture into four portions, then roll each into a ball and shape into patties.

3. Heat a large skillet or grill pan over medium-high heat. Place the burgers in the skillet and cook for 4 minutes. Flip the burgers over and add a slice of cheese to each. Continue cooking for 4 minutes more, until the cheese is melted and the burgers are done.

4. Lay out the burger buns on a flat work surface, then slather with Dijon mustard. Assemble the burgers starting with the bun bottom and layering on the cheeseburger, 2 tablespoons of green chiles, and the bun top.

Per Serving: Calories: 427; Fat: 9g; Carbohydrates: 42g; Protein: 45g; Fiber: 12g; Sodium: 1,294mg

Caprese Burgers

PREP TIME: 15 minutes
COOK TIME: 15 minutes
SERVES 4

Generally speaking, I am not a salad person, but salad in the form of a burger? Now you're speaking my language! Fresh basil and tomatoes make this a great summertime burger.

4 large tomato slices (½ inch thick)

1 tablespoon balsamic vinegar

1 tablespoon olive oil

⅛ teaspoon salt

½ teaspoon plus ⅛ teaspoon freshly ground black pepper

½ cup vegan mayonnaise

¼ cup vegan pesto

24 ounces vegan ground beef

½ cup shredded vegan Parmesan cheese

¼ cup finely chopped fresh basil, plus more leaves for serving

1 tablespoon tomato paste

1 teaspoon minced garlic

4 slices vegan mozzarella cheese (½ inch thick)

4 vegan hamburger buns, lightly toasted

1. Into a shallow dish, place the tomato slices in an even layer. In a small bowl, whisk together the balsamic vinegar, oil, salt, and ⅛ teaspoon of black pepper. Pour the vinaigrette over the tomato slices and set aside.

2. In a separate small bowl, stir together the mayonnaise and pesto. Set aside.

3. In a large bowl, combine the vegan ground beef, vegan Parmesan, basil, tomato paste, garlic, and remaining ½ teaspoon of black pepper. Mix together to incorporate. Divide the mixture into four portions. Roll each portion into a ball, then shape into patties.

4. Heat a large skillet or grill pan over medium-high heat. Place the burgers in the skillet and cook for 4 minutes. Flip the burgers over and add a slice of mozzarella. Continue cooking for 4 minutes more, until the cheese is softened and the burgers are done.

5. To build the burgers, spread pesto mayo on the bun bottoms, then top with patties, marinated tomato slices, fresh basil leaves, and the bun tops. Serve.

Per Serving: Calories: 770; Fat: 37g; Carbohydrates: 54g; Protein: 54g; Fiber: 12g; Sodium: 1,920mg

Barbecue Burgers

When it comes to barbeque, there is no shortage of strong opinions about which style of sauce reigns supreme. Texas, Kansas City, Memphis, South Carolina, North Carolina, Alabama, and Kentucky . . . each one has its merits. With such a wide variety of regional sauces on the market today, it's easy to customize these burgers to suit your taste.

24 ounces vegan ground beef

1 cup barbecue sauce, divided

1 teaspoon onion powder

⅔ teaspoon garlic powder

1 teaspoon salt

½ teaspoon freshly ground black pepper

4 vegan hamburger buns

Yellow mustard, for topping (optional)

Green-leaf lettuce, for topping (optional)

Vegan Cheddar cheese, for topping (optional)

Sliced tomatoes, for topping (optional)

Fresh or pickled jalapeño peppers, for topping (optional)

1. In a large bowl, mix together the vegan ground beef, ½ cup of barbecue sauce, onion powder, garlic powder, salt, and black pepper. Divide the mixture into four portions. Roll each portion into a ball and shape into patties.

2. Heat a large skillet or grill pan over medium-high heat. Place the patties in the skillet and cook for 4 minutes on each side, basting with additional sauce.

3. To build the burgers, spread each half of the buns with mustard, then layer the bottom half with lettuce, a burger patty, cheese, tomato, and jalapeños (or the toppings of your choosing). Cover with the bun tops, then serve.

INGREDIENT TIP: For a fun twist, try experimenting with the unique flavor profiles of international-style barbecue sauces, such as Korean-style, Caribbean-style, and Thai-style.

Per Serving: Calories: 644; Fat: 8g; Carbohydrates: 97g; Protein: 47g; Fiber: 14g; Sodium: 1,904mg

Juicy Lucys

At first glance, the Minneapolis-born Juicy Lucy may look a bit unremarkable, but the beauty of this "meaty" and molten cheese-stuffed burger lies in its simplicity. One bite and you'll be hooked. Try it with different types of vegan cheeses, such as mozzarella, pepper Jack, provolone, or Gouda. Just be sure to let the burgers rest for a few minutes before biting into them because the cheese will be hot! You can add toppings to these burgers if you want, but they're not really necessary.

24 ounces vegan ground beef

1 tablespoon vegan Worcestershire sauce (see Ingredient Tip)

1 teaspoon garlic salt

½ teaspoon freshly ground black pepper

8 slices vegan American-style cheese slices

Salt

4 vegan hamburger buns

1. In a large bowl, mix together the vegan ground beef, Worcestershire, garlic salt, and black pepper. Divide the mixture into four portions, then again into eight. Roll each portion into a ball, then shape into thin patties.

2. Arrange the patties on a flat work surface. Top each with 2 slices of cheese, tearing the cheese as needed so that it fits on the patty with no overhang. Cover with a second patty and shape the meat around the cheese to fully enclose it. Season both sides of the patties with salt and black pepper.

3. Heat a large skillet or grill pan over medium-high heat. Place the patties in the skillet and cook for 4 minutes on each side.

4. To assemble the burgers, simply sandwich the patties between soft burger buns and tuck in!

INGREDIENT TIP: Traditional Worcestershire sauce frequently contains anchovies. Thankfully, there are several vegan options available. Look for vegan Worcestershire sauce in the organic specialty foods section of your supermarket.

Per Serving: Calories: 461; Fat: 11g; Carbohydrates: 41g; Protein: 47g; Fiber: 11g; Sodium: 1,575mg

"Sausage" and Peppers Pasta // p. 61

Chapter 5

STOVE TOP SATISFACTION

Salisbury "Steak" with Mushroom Gravy

PREP TIME: 10 minutes
COOK TIME: 45 minutes
SERVES 4

Forget what you may know of Salisbury steak from TV dinners past; this dish of tender vegan ground beef patties smothered in rich and creamy gravy is pure American-style, stick-to-your-ribs comfort food.

Fun fact: Salisbury steak is named for a 19th-century American physician who actually recommended eating the meal up to three times a day. Seems a bit excessive to me, but hey, you do you, boo.

16 ounces vegan ground beef

½ cup seasoned bread crumbs

2 tablespoons mild-flavored plant milk (such as oat or unsweetened almond)

1 (2-ounce) package dry onion soup mix, divided

2 teaspoons vegan Worcestershire sauce

¼ teaspoon freshly ground black pepper, plus more for seasoning

3 tablespoons vegan butter

8 ounces cremini mushrooms, stemmed and thinly sliced

½ cup thinly sliced yellow onion

1 teaspoon minced garlic

3 tablespoons all-purpose flour

2½ cups vegan beef-style broth

Salt

1. In a large bowl, mix together the vegan ground beef, bread crumbs, milk, half the onion soup mix, Worcestershire sauce, and black pepper. Divide the mixture into four portions, then form into patties.

2. Line a plate with paper towels.

3. Heat a large skillet over medium-high heat. Place the patties in the skillet and cook for 4 minutes per side. Transfer the cooked patties to the prepared plate and set aside.

4. Keep the skillet on medium-high heat and add the butter. When the butter is melted, add the mushrooms and onion. Cook for 3 minutes, stirring frequently, until tender. Add the garlic and continue cooking for 1 minute more.

5. Whisk in the flour and the remaining onion soup mix. Gradually add the broth, stirring continuously. Turn down the heat to medium and continue cooking for 3 minutes, until thickened. Season to taste with salt and pepper.

6. Return the patties to the skillet with the gravy. Reduce the heat to low and simmer for 30 minutes, then serve.

Per Serving: Calories: 324; Fat: 11g; Carbohydrates: 29g; Protein: 25g; Fiber: 8g; Sodium: 694mg

Black Pepper "Chicken" Stir-Fry

In less time than it takes to get takeout, you can whip up this easy, one-skillet dinner. I love that this recipe is super forgiving, too. You can use pretty much whatever veggies you have sitting around, which is great for when groceries are running low.

¼ cup tamari

1 tablespoon rice wine vinegar

1 tablespoon cornstarch

1 tablespoon coarsely ground black pepper

1 teaspoon grated fresh ginger

2 tablespoons peanut oil

20 ounces vegan chicken-style strips

2 cups snow peas

1 cup shredded green cabbage

1 cup thinly sliced red bell pepper

½ cup thinly sliced celery

½ cup thinly sliced yellow onion

Rice or noodles, for serving (optional)

1. In a small bowl, whisk together the tamari, vinegar, cornstarch, black pepper, and ginger to make a sauce. Set aside.

2. Heat the oil in a wok or large deep skillet over medium-high heat. Carefully add the chicken strips and cook for 5 minutes, turning frequently, until browned on all sides. Transfer the vegan chicken to a cutting board and slice into 1-inch pieces.

3. Into the hot pan, add the snow peas, cabbage, bell pepper, celery, and onion. Cook for 3 minutes, until the vegetables are crisp-tender.

4. Return the vegan chicken to the pan with the vegetables, then pour in the sauce. Stir to coat the vegan chicken and vegetables and continue cooking for 2 minutes, until heated through.

5. Spoon the black pepper "chicken" stir-fry over rice or noodles and serve.

Per Serving: Calories: 430; Fat: 25g; Carbohydrates: 15g; Protein: 37g; Fiber: 8g; Sodium: 1,828mg

Tacos al Pastor

The term "al pastor" refers to thinly sliced meat—usually pork but it can also be chicken or beef—that has been marinated in a citrus-based sauce and grilled to perfection. Heads up! The vegan pork used in this recipe needs to be marinated for at least 2 hours, so plan accordingly.

20 ounces vegan pork meat, thawed (such as Gardein Porkless Bites; discard sauce packet, if included)

2 cups small bite-size chunks fresh pineapple, divided

¼ cup chopped white onion

¼ cup freshly squeezed orange juice

2 tablespoons distilled white vinegar

1 tablespoon ancho chile powder

2 teaspoons minced garlic

¾ teaspoon salt

½ teaspoon Mexican oregano

1 chipotle pepper in adobo sauce

1 tablespoon vegetable oil

8 (5-inch) street taco–size flour tortillas

Chopped cilantro, for serving

Thinly sliced red onion, for serving

1 lime, quartered

1. Cut the vegan pork meat into thin slices and set in a medium bowl.

2. In a blender, combine ½ cup of pineapple chunks, the onion, orange juice, vinegar, chile powder, garlic, salt, oregano, and chipotle pepper. Blend until the consistency is very smooth. Pour the marinade over the "pork" slices, then refrigerate, covered, for 2 hours.

3. Heat the oil in a large skillet or grill pan over medium-high heat. When the oil is hot, remove the vegan pork slices from the marinade, shaking off any excess, and carefully place them in the skillet. Add the remaining 1½ cups of pineapple. Cook for 10 minutes, turning occasionally, until the "pork" and pineapple are seared.

4. Spoon into warm tortillas, top with cilantro and red onion, and serve with a wedge of lime.

Per Serving: Calories: 589; Fat: 25g; Carbohydrates: 52g; Protein: 39g; Fiber: 8g; Sodium: 1,870mg

Pesto Spaghetti and "Meatballs"

Every year, my husband plants a garden and includes my favorite cooking herbs. Basil is always among my top requests. By the end of summer, the plants are enormous, and one of my favorite ways to use our abundance of fresh basil is by making pesto. It's so quick and easy to make and really gives this pasta a lightness that is a nice complement to the seasonings of the vegan meatballs.

12 vegan meatballs

2 cups packed fresh basil leaves

2 tablespoons pine nuts

2 teaspoons minced garlic

½ cup olive oil

½ cup grated vegan Parmesan cheese, plus more for serving

½ teaspoon salt

¼ teaspoon freshly ground black pepper

16 ounces spaghetti pasta

1. Cook the vegan meatballs according to the package directions. Set aside.

2. While the meatballs are cooking, make the pesto. In a food processor, combine the basil leaves, pine nuts, and garlic. Pulse until coarsely chopped. Add the olive oil, cheese, salt, and black pepper. Blend until the mixture is well blended but still has some texture. Set aside.

3. Cook the pasta according to the package directions, reserving 1 cup of the cooking water prior to draining in a colander. Turn off the heat.

4. Return the drained spaghetti to the cooking pot. Add the pesto and ½ cup of reserved water, adding more as needed and tossing gently to coat the pasta completely.

5. To serve, scoop spaghetti into large pasta bowls, then top with the vegan meatballs and Parmesan cheese.

COOKING TIP: Got a garden bursting with basil? Make a double (or triple!) batch of pesto and store it for later. Fresh pesto should always be stored in an airtight container. It will keep well in the refrigerator for up to 3 days or, for longer-term storage, up to 6 months in the freezer.

Per Serving: Calories: 384; Fat: 7g; Carbohydrates: 40g; Protein: 20g; Fiber: 5g; Sodium: 1,370mg

"Bacon" Fried Rice

PREP TIME: 1 hour 10 minutes

COOK TIME: 25 minutes

SERVES 4

It's true what they say: Vegan bacon makes everything better. At least I think that's how the saying goes, anyway. For this recipe, bacon definitely elevates everyday fried rice to a whole new and deliciously smoky level.

1 cup jasmine rice

2 cups water

6 slices vegan bacon, roughly chopped

1 cup frozen peas

½ cup chopped sweet yellow onion

½ cup shredded carrots

1 teaspoon freshly grated ginger

1 tablespoon tamari or soy sauce

1 teaspoon sriracha

½ teaspoon toasted sesame oil

¼ cup thinly sliced scallions

1. In a medium saucepan, combine the rice and water. Bring to a boil, then turn down the heat to low. Simmer for 15 minutes, until the liquid has been absorbed and the rice is tender. Transfer to a bowl and let cool in the refrigerator for at least 1 hour.

2. Line a plate with paper towels.

3. In a large, deep skillet, cook the vegan bacon according to the package directions. Transfer to the prepared plate. Do not wipe out the skillet.

4. Into the skillet over medium heat, add the peas, onion, carrots, and ginger. Cook for 2 minutes, stirring frequently.

5. Add the cold rice to the vegetables. Use a spatula to break up any clumps of rice. Cook for 5 minutes, until the rice is heated through, stirring halfway through the cooking time.

6. Add the tamari, sriracha, sesame oil, and vegan bacon to the rice and stir to coat.

7. Spoon into bowls, garnish with the scallions, and serve.

INGREDIENT TIP: Jasmine rice, with its lightly aromatic quality and resistance to clumping, is a classic choice for fried rice. However, if jasmine rice is not available, whatever long-grain or medium-grain rice you have on hand will work just fine.

Per Serving: Calories: 248; Fat: 3g; Carbohydrates: 47g; Protein: 7g; Fiber: 4g; Sodium: 378mg

"Meatball" Curry

PREP TIME: 15 minutes

COOK TIME: 50 minutes

SERVES 4 TO 6

Let's talk about curries. Contrary to popular opinion, a curry is not a singular type of dish or flavor profile. Although curry powder is a commonly used blend of spices, it is not a required ingredient for a dish to be considered a curry. Curry simply means "sauce or gravy." Curry dishes have a strong association with Indian-style fare, but they are also popular in Japanese, Filipino, and Thai cuisine as well as many other countries throughout Asia. This particular recipe is made in the Indian style of curry with ginger and curry powder–spiced meatballs simmered in a creamy coconut sauce.

24 ounces vegan ground beef

4 tablespoons finely chopped fresh cilantro, divided

4 teaspoons minced fresh ginger, divided

2 tablespoons plus 2 teaspoons curry powder

1 teaspoon salt

¼ teaspoon freshly ground black pepper

3 tablespoons unrefined coconut oil

½ cup chopped shallots

1 tablespoon minced garlic

1 (14-ounce) can petite tomatoes, with juices

1 cup fresh spinach, chopped

14 ounces unsweetened coconut milk

1 teaspoon garam masala

Rice, for serving (optional)

1. Preheat the oven to 375°F.

2. In a large bowl, mix together the vegan ground beef, 2 tablespoons of cilantro, 2 teaspoons of ginger, 2 teaspoons of curry powder, the salt, and black pepper. Divide the mixture into four portions, then roll each portion into 6 meatballs so that you have 24 meatballs total. Arrange the meatballs on a baking sheet at least 1 inch apart. Bake for 20 minutes, then set aside.

3. Heat the coconut oil in a large, deep skillet over medium heat. When the oil is hot, add the shallots, garlic, and the remaining 2 teaspoons of ginger. Cook for 2 minutes, stirring frequently, until the shallot is softened and the garlic is very lightly golden in color. Add the remaining 2 tablespoons of curry powder and stir to coat.

4. Add the tomatoes and spinach. Cook for 2 minutes, until the spinach has wilted.

5. Stir in the coconut milk and garam masala. Turn down the heat to low and simmer for 20 minutes.

6. Add the meatballs, turning to coat them in the sauce, and cook for 5 minutes more until the meatballs are heated through. Garnish with the remaining 2 tablespoons of cilantro and serve over rice, if desired.

INGREDIENT TIP: Look for garam masala powder in the Indian specialty aisle of your supermarket. You can add up to 3 teaspoons depending on your spice preference.

Per Serving: Calories: 556; Fat: 36g; Carbohydrates: 24g; Protein: 40g; Fiber: 13g; Sodium: 1,434mg

"Turkey" Piccata

PREP TIME: 5 minutes
COOK TIME: 25 minutes
SERVES 4

This is a nice dish to serve when having people over for dinner. These breaded vegan turkey cutlets in a light and lemony wine sauce are elegant enough for company yet easy enough for every day. I like to round out the meal with mashed potatoes and steamed green beans.

8 breaded vegan turkey cutlets (such as Gardein Turk'y Cutlets; discard the gravy packet, if included)

4 tablespoons (½ stick) vegan butter

½ cup dry white wine

½ cup vegan chicken-style broth

2 tablespoons freshly squeezed lemon juice

1 tablespoon minced fresh parsley, plus more for garnish

1 tablespoon capers, coarsely chopped

⅛ teaspoon freshly ground black pepper

1. Bake the vegan turkey cutlets according to the package directions and set aside.

2. In a large skillet over medium heat, heat the butter. When the butter is melted, pour in the wine and broth. Bring to a boil and cook for 3 minutes.

3. Turn down the heat to low, then add the lemon juice, parsley, and capers. Whisk to combine and continue cooking for 3 minutes.

4. Spoon the sauce over the vegan turkey cutlets. Season with black pepper, then garnish with additional parsley and serve.

Per Serving: Calories: 295; Fat: 18g; Carbohydrates: 18g; Protein: 14g; Fiber: 0g; Sodium: 590mg

"Sausage" and Peppers Pasta

Sausage and peppers are practically made for each other. If you want to go lower-carb on this dish, you could technically serve the vegan sausage and peppers on their own and omit the pasta entirely. You won't see *me* doing that, though; pass the pasta!

8 ounces farfalle pasta or your favorite medium shape

1 tablespoon olive oil

7 ounces vegan hot Italian-style sausage links, cut into medallions

6 medium red, orange, and yellow bell peppers

¼ cup diced yellow onion

3 garlic cloves, minced

1 (14-ounce) can diced tomatoes with liquid

1½ teaspoons dried basil

1½ teaspoons dried oregano

1 teaspoon salt

½ teaspoon freshly ground black pepper

¼ teaspoon red pepper flakes

1. Cook the pasta according to the package directions for al dente consistency. Drain and set aside.

2. Line a plate with paper towels.

3. While the pasta is cooking, heat the olive oil in a large, deep skillet over medium heat. When the oil is hot, add the vegan sausage. Cook for 5 minutes, stirring frequently, until heated through and browned on both sides. Transfer the cooked sausage to the prepared plate.

4. In the same skillet, cook the bell peppers and onion for 3 minutes, stirring frequently, until softened. Add the garlic and continue cooking for 1 minute more.

5. Return the vegan sausage to the skillet with the vegetables. Add the diced tomatoes with their juices, the basil, oregano, salt, black pepper, and red pepper flakes. Stir to combine. Cook for 5 minutes.

6. Stir the cooked pasta into the mixture in the skillet. Turn down the heat to medium-low, cover the pan, and allow to simmer for 5 minutes. Spoon into pasta bowls and serve.

Per Serving: Calories: 473; Fat: 15g; Carbohydrates: 69g; Protein: 20g; Fiber: 9g; Sodium: 1,576mg

Teriyaki "Meatball" Rice Bowls

If you love sweet and savory together in one bite, have I got a dish for you. The fresh flavors of ginger, garlic, and scallions really shine through in these juicy and tender "meatballs," while the homemade teriyaki sauce offers a slight sweetness to balance out the dish. This recipe is pretty versatile, too. Sometimes I serve the meatballs on their own as an easy appetizer. Keep in mind that the "meatballs" need at least an hour to chill in the refrigerator, so plan accordingly!

1 cup uncooked jasmine rice

2 cups plus 3 tablespoons water

½ teaspoon garlic salt

¼ teaspoon freshly ground black pepper

12 ounces vegan ground beef

¼ cup finely chopped scallions

2 teaspoons crushed ginger paste

2 teaspoons minced garlic

1 teaspoon salt

1 tablespoon toasted sesame oil

3 tablespoons tamari or soy sauce

2 tablespoons vegan honey

1 tablespoon rice vinegar

½ teaspoon cornstarch

2 tablespoons chopped scallions, for garnish

1 teaspoon sesame seeds, toasted, for garnish

1. Combine the rice and 2 cups of water in a medium saucepan. Bring to a boil, then turn down the heat to low. Simmer for 15 minutes, until the liquid has been absorbed and the rice is tender. Season with the garlic salt and black pepper. Set aside.

2. In a medium bowl, mix together the vegan ground beef, scallions, ginger paste, garlic, and salt. Form the mixture into 20 equal meatballs. Chill in the refrigerator for at least 1 hour and up to overnight.

3. In a large skillet over medium heat, heat the sesame oil. When the oil is hot, add the meatballs in an even layer. Cook for about 7 minutes, shaking the skillet frequently to turn the meatballs, until the meatballs are browned and cooked through. Transfer the meatballs to a plate and wipe out the skillet.

4. In the skillet, whisk together the tamari, 3 tablespoons of water, the honey, rice vinegar, and cornstarch. Add the meatballs, turning them to coat. Cook for 1 minute, until the sauce is slightly thickened.

5. Spoon the rice into bowls and top with the meatballs. Garnish with the sliced scallions and toasted sesame seeds.

INGREDIENT TIPS: You can't beat homemade sauce, but ½ cup of good-quality store-bought teriyaki sauce will work in a pinch.

There are lots of plant-based honeys on the market; any will work for this recipe. Look for vegan honey in the plant-based specialty foods aisle of your supermarket. If it's not available in your area, agave nectar works just fine.

Per Serving: Calories: 373; Fat: 6g; Carbohydrates: 56g; Protein: 23g; Fiber: 7g; Sodium: 1,660mg

Low Country Boil

PREP TIME: 10 minutes
COOK TIME: 25 minutes
SERVES 4

Get out your big pot and cover the picnic table in newspaper because we're about to get down and dirty with a good old-fashioned, roll-up-your-sleeves, eat-with-your-hands Southern-style boil. Serve this vegan rendition of the classic Low Country feast with a nice crusty bread for sopping up the sauce.

8 tablespoons (1 stick) plus 1 tablespoon vegan butter, divided

16 ounces vegan sausage, cut into 2-inch pieces

1 sweet yellow onion, cut into 6 wedges

1 (12-ounce) bottle pale ale beer

10 cups water

1 pound baby red potatoes

1 (3-ounce) bag seafood boil spice mix

2 bay leaves

4 ears corn, husked and cut into 2-inch pieces

½ pound green beans, trimmed

2 tablespoons finely chopped fresh parsley

1 teaspoon minced garlic

½ teaspoon freshly ground black pepper

¼ teaspoon salt

1. Melt 1 tablespoon of butter in a large stockpot over medium heat. Add the sausage and onion. Cook for 6 minutes, until the sausage slices are browned on both sides. Transfer the sausage to a plate and set aside.

2. Into the same pot, add the beer, water, potatoes, spice mix bag, and bay leaves. Cover the pot and bring to a rolling boil for 8 minutes, until the potatoes are almost fork-tender.

3. Carefully add the corn and continue boiling for 5 minutes. Add the green beans and boil for 5 minutes more, until crisp-tender. Return the sausage to the pot, then immediately drain in a colander.

4. In a small saucepan over medium heat, melt the remaining 8 tablespoons of butter. Stir in the parsley, garlic, black pepper, and salt.

5. To serve, pile the Low Country boil onto a large serving platter, or pour it out directly onto the paper-covered table. Drizzle with the garlic butter and dig in!

Per Serving: Calories: 776; Fat: 45g; Carbohydrates: 71g; Protein: 30g; Fiber: 11g; Sodium: 1,429mg

Pulled "Pork" Hash

PREP TIME: 5 minutes

COOK TIME: 30 minutes

SERVES 4

In its most basic form, hash consists of meat, potatoes, and onions. If that sounds boring to you, then we are in agreement, my friend. For this recipe, we're improving on the base by adding colorful veggies, savory seasonings, vegan egg replacer, and dairy-free Cheddar cheese. Serve with a simple green salad and toast for an easy, one-skillet meal that is right at home at breakfast, brunch, or breakfast-for-dinner night.

10 ounces vegan pork shreds

2 teaspoons vegan butter

¼ cup chopped red onion

¼ cup chopped orange
   bell pepper

¼ teaspoon salt

¼ teaspoon freshly ground
   black pepper

⅛ teaspoon cayenne pepper

15 ounces shredded hash
   browns, thawed and
   patted dry

¼ cup liquid vegan egg
   substitute (such as
   JUST Egg)

½ cup shredded vegan
   Cheddar cheese

1. Cook the vegan pork shreds according to the package directions. Transfer to a cutting board and roughly chop.

2. In a large, deep skillet over medium heat, melt the butter. Add the onion and bell pepper and cook, stirring frequently, for 2 minutes. Add the vegan pork, salt, black pepper, and cayenne pepper. Continue cooking for 2 minutes more.

3. Stir in the hash browns and spread into an even layer in the pan. Cook undisturbed for 5 minutes to lightly brown, then turn the hash browns. Cook for another 5 minutes to brown the other side.

4. Pour the liquid vegan egg over the hash browns. Cook undisturbed for 3 minutes, until the eggs are done.

5. Sprinkle the cheese over the top. Turn down the heat to low. Cover the pan for 3 minutes to melt the cheese, then serve.

Per Serving: Calories: 342; Fat: 15g; Carbohydrates: 27g; Protein: 25g; Fiber: 4g; Sodium: 1,095mg

"Chicken" and "Chorizo" Paella

PREP TIME: 10 minutes
COOK TIME: 35 minutes
SERVES 4

Vegan chorizo-style sausage is uniquely smoky and highly seasoned. Its bold flavor profile is exactly what makes vegan chorizo the ideal choice for this Spanish-influenced paella. This dish is a hearty meal unto itself with a lot going on in it, so if you're inclined to add a side, I would keep it simple with a light salad or a nice bowl of olives.

3 tablespoons olive oil, divided

10 ounces vegan chicken-style strips, cut into 1-inch pieces

2 teaspoons smoked paprika

½ teaspoon salt

¼ teaspoon freshly ground black pepper

12 ounces vegan chorizo-style sausage links, cut into 1-inch rounds

½ cup diced red bell pepper

¼ cup diced yellow onion

1 tablespoon minced garlic

3 cups vegan chicken-style broth

12 saffron threads

1¾ cups short-grain rice (such as Valencia, Arborio, or Bomba)

1 cup frozen peas, thawed

1. In a large, deep skillet or paella pan over medium-high heat, heat 2 tablespoons of olive oil. When the oil is hot, add the vegan chicken. Season with the paprika, salt, and black pepper. Cook for 5 minutes, turning the strips to brown on both sides. Transfer the strips to a cutting board and cut into 1-inch pieces. Do not wipe out the skillet.

2. Add the sausage to the skillet and cook for 5 minutes, turning to brown it on both sides. Transfer the cooked sausage slices to the cutting board with the "chicken."

3. In the same skillet, heat the remaining 1 tablespoon of olive oil. When the oil is hot, add the bell pepper and onion. Cook for 2 minutes, until softened. Add the garlic and continue cooking for 1 minute more.

4. Add the broth, saffron, and rice. Give the rice one good stir around the skillet, just enough to cover it completely with the liquid. Bring to a low boil, then turn down the heat to low. Cover and simmer for 15 minutes, until the rice is cooked.

5. Gently stir in the vegan chicken, sausage, and peas. Continue cooking undisturbed for 5 minutes more to get a light crust on the bottom of the rice, then serve.

INGREDIENT TIP: Short-grain rice is essential to a great paella. It can absorb more liquid than long grain without getting mushy, resulting in the drier texture needed to get a perfectly light crust on the bottom.

Per Serving: Calories: 829; Fat: 36g; Carbohydrates: 88g; Protein: 41g; Fiber: 10g; Sodium: 1,554mg

Loaded "Chicken" Nachos // p. 84

LOVIN' FROM THE VEGAN OVEN

"Chicken" Pot Pie

Frozen chicken pot pies were on regular rotation in my house back when I was a kid in the 1970s and were usually consumed in front of the TV. I thought they were pretty great. Thankfully, my tastes and preferences have evolved to include this upgraded and modern vegan version.

2 tablespoons olive oil

9 ounces vegan
chicken-style strips

1 cup sliced carrots

½ cup sliced celery

1 teaspoon poultry
seasoning blend

1 teaspoon freshly ground black
pepper, divided

¼ teaspoon garlic powder

1 cup frozen peas

⅔ cup vegan butter

⅔ cup diced yellow onion

⅓ cup all-purpose flour

1 teaspoon salt

½ teaspoon celery seed

3½ cups vegan
chicken-style broth

1¼ cups mild-flavored
plant milk (such as oat or
unsweetened almond)

2 (9-inch) frozen deep-dish pie
crusts, thawed

1. Preheat the oven to 375°F.

2. In a large skillet over medium-high heat, heat the oil. When the oil is hot, add the vegan chicken strips. Cook for 3 minutes, turning frequently, until browned.

3. Stir in the carrots and celery, then sprinkle with the poultry seasoning, ½ teaspoon of black pepper, and garlic powder. Continue cooking for 5 minutes, stirring frequently, until the vegetables are fork-tender. Add the peas and continue cooking for 2 minutes more to heat through. Remove from the heat and transfer to a medium bowl.

4. In the same skillet over medium-high heat, melt the butter. When the butter is melted, add the onion. Cook for 2 minutes, until softened. Turn down the heat to low.

5. Whisk in the flour, salt, the remaining ½ teaspoon of black pepper, and the celery seed to make a roux. Gradually pour in the broth and milk, whisking constantly to incorporate. Simmer for 3 minutes, stirring frequently, until thickened. Remove from the heat.

6. Stir in the vegan chicken and vegetable mixture, then pour into one of the pie crusts. Remove the remaining pie crust from its tin and place it over the filled crust to cover the contents completely, pinching the dough around the rim to seal the edges. Cut four 2-inch slits in the top crust.

7. Set the filled pie on a baking sheet and bake for 45 minutes, until the pie crust is golden brown. Allow to cool for 10 minutes before serving.

Per Serving: Calories: 1,085; Fat: 75g; Carbohydrates: 76g; Protein: 27g; Fiber: 8g; Sodium: 1,755mg

Mini "Meat" Loaves

PREP TIME: 10 minutes

COOK TIME: 55 minutes

SERVES 4

These mini vegan meat loaves are an excellent choice for busy weeknights. I like that the individual serving portions cook faster than a full-size meat loaf, giving you all the comfort-food deliciousness in a fraction of the time.

Nonstick cooking spray

12 ounces vegan ground beef

1 cup plus 2 tablespoons Italian-seasoned bread crumbs

½ cup tomato-based ketchup, divided

3 garlic cloves, minced

1 tablespoon vegan concentrated beef-style bouillon base

¼ teaspoon onion powder

¼ teaspoon freshly ground black pepper

⅛ teaspoon celery salt

⅛ teaspoon paprika

2 tablespoons vegetable oil

1. Preheat the oven to 350°F. Spray an 8½-by-11-inch baking dish with cooking spray.

2. In a large bowl, mix together the vegan ground beef, bread crumbs, ¼ cup of ketchup, garlic, bouillon base, onion powder, black pepper, celery salt, and paprika. Divide the mixture into four portions, then form each portion into a loaf shape.

3. In a large skillet over medium-high heat, heat the oil. When the oil is hot, place each vegan meat loaf into the skillet. Cook for 8 minutes, turning to brown each side.

4. Arrange the meat loaves in the prepared baking dish. Bake for 20 minutes, or until the internal temperature reaches 160°F. Brush the loaves with the remaining ¼ cup of ketchup and return them to the oven for 5 minutes more. Allow to stand for 10 minutes, then slice and serve.

EQUIPMENT TIP: Meat thermometers aren't just for meat eaters, and every plant-based kitchen should have one. A quick and easy way to tell if your "meat" loaves are done is to stick a thermometer directly into the center. When the food is fully cooked, the thermometer should indicate an internal temperature of 160°F.

Per Serving: Calories: 270; Fat: 10g; Carbohydrates: 26g; Protein: 20g; Fiber: 6g; Sodium: 732mg

"Beefy" Bean and Cheese Enchiladas

Just a handful of ingredients are all you need to whip up these flavorful Tex-Mex-style enchiladas. Round out the meal with sides of rice and a simple salad, and dinner is set.

Nonstick cooking spray

2 tablespoons olive oil

12 ounces vegan ground beef

¼ cup diced yellow onion

1 (15-ounce) can vegan refried beans

1 tablespoon taco seasoning blend

2 cups shredded vegan Cheddar cheese, divided

8 medium flour tortillas

12 ounces red enchilada sauce

1. Preheat the oven to 350°F. Spray a 9-by-13-inch baking dish with cooking spray.

2. In a large skillet over medium-high heat, heat the olive oil. When the oil is hot, add the vegan ground beef and onion. Cook for 5 minutes, stirring frequently, until the "beef" is browned and the onion is softened.

3. Stir in the refried beans and taco seasoning blend. Continue cooking for 3 minutes more, stirring frequently. Remove from the heat and stir in 1 cup of cheese.

4. Spoon a generous amount of filling in a line down the center of 1 tortilla. Roll the tortilla and place seam-side down in the prepared baking dish. Repeat with the remaining filling and tortillas.

5. Pour the enchilada sauce over the top of the enchiladas to cover. Sprinkle with the remaining 1 cup of cheese. Cover and bake for 40 minutes.

6. Use a wide spatula to lift the enchiladas out of the pan and onto plates, then serve.

Per Serving: Calories: 890; Fat: 32g; Carbohydrates: 91g; Protein: 52g; Fiber: 14g; Sodium: 1,960mg

Buffalo "Chicken" Pizza

PREP TIME: 5 minutes

COOK TIME: 15 minutes

SERVES 4

Back in the day when I worked as a hostess at Mario's Flying Pizza on Seawall Boulevard in Galveston, Texas, I used to love watching the cooks in the open kitchen as they tossed the pizza dough into the air. They would send the dough soaring and spinning until it was the perfect size. Pizza dough tossing is a skill I never mastered, but it sure was fun to watch. I think of Mario's every time I make pizza at home.

3 tablespoons vegan butter, divided

2 tablespoons Buffalo-style wing sauce

10 ounces vegan chicken-style strips

1 (12-inch) prepared pizza crust

¼ cup vegan blue cheese dressing

¾ cup shredded vegan mozzarella cheese, divided

¾ cup shredded vegan Cheddar cheese, divided

2 tablespoons thinly sliced red onion

2 tablespoons thinly sliced celery

1. Preheat the oven to 425°F.

2. In a medium bowl, melt 2 tablespoons of vegan butter in the microwave. Add the Buffalo sauce and stir to combine.

3. In a large skillet over medium-high heat, melt the remaining 1 tablespoon of butter. When the butter is melted, add the vegan chicken strips. Cook for 5 minutes, turning frequently, until browned. Transfer the strips to a cutting board and cut into ½-inch pieces. Place the vegan chicken into the bowl with the butter and Buffalo sauce. Toss to coat.

4. Set the pizza crust on a pizza stone or baking sheet. Brush the blue cheese dressing onto the crust, leaving a 1-inch border around the edge. Layer with ½ cup of mozzarella, ½ cup of Cheddar, and the red onion, celery, and "chicken." Top with the remaining ¼ cup of mozzarella and remaining ¼ cup of Cheddar.

5. Bake for 10 minutes, until the cheeses are melted, then slice and serve.

Per Serving: Calories: 778; Fat: 39g; Carbohydrates: 66g; Protein: 41g; Fiber: 6g; Sodium: 1,987mg

Red Rice and "Sausage" Casserole

PREP TIME: 5 minutes

COOK TIME: 1 hour 20 minutes

SERVES 6

Red rice, also known as Charleston red rice, is especially popular in its namesake area of South Carolina. I like this simple Southern-style classic for its balance of spicy and slightly sweet that comes from the vegan sausage, Cajun seasonings, and tomato-based rice. Collard greens and corn bread pair well with this dish.

Nonstick cooking spray

1 tablespoon vegan butter

28 ounces hot Italian-style sausage, cut into ½-inch pieces

½ cup diced green bell pepper

½ cup diced yellow onion

½ cup diced celery

1 teaspoon minced garlic

2 cups long-grain rice

1 (28-ounce) can petite diced tomatoes, with liquid

1 tablespoon Cajun seasoning

1 teaspoon salt

½ teaspoon freshly ground black pepper

1 cup water

1. Preheat the oven to 375°F. Spray an 8-by-11-inch baking dish with cooking spray.

2. In a large skillet over medium-high heat, melt the butter. When the butter is melted, add the sausage, bell pepper, onion, and celery. Cook for 5 minutes, until the sausage is browned. Add the garlic and cook for 1 minute more.

3. Mix in the rice and cook for 1 minute, stirring frequently to very lightly toast the rice. Add the tomatoes with their liquid, the Cajun seasoning, salt, and black pepper.

4. Pour into the prepared baking dish. Pour in the water, stirring to distribute it throughout the casserole. Cover tightly with foil.

5. Bake for 1 hour and 15 minutes, until the rice is fully cooked. Fluff the rice with a fork and serve.

INGREDIENT TIP: Creole seasoning has a similar flavor profile to Cajun seasoning and can be used as a substitute in a pinch.

Per Serving: Calories: 616; Fat: 26g; Carbohydrates: 70g; Protein: 30g; Fiber: 8g; Sodium: 1,706mg

Ground "Beef" Wellington with Mushroom Gravy

PREP TIME: 15 minutes
COOK TIME: 1 hour
SERVES 4

This vegan spin on the classic dinner roast takes a little extra time, but the effort is well worth it. The presentation of this savory Wellington, with its pretty patterned layering of puff pastry dough, qualifies it for a place on the holiday table or date night at home.

FOR THE "BEEF" WELLINGTON

12 ounces vegan ground beef

2 cups finely chopped cremini mushrooms

½ cup finely chopped yellow onion

½ cup small-diced carrot

⅓ teaspoon dried rosemary

⅓ teaspoon dried thyme

¼ teaspoon salt

¼ teaspoon freshly ground black pepper

1 tablespoon minced garlic

½ cup vegan beef-style broth

1½ tablespoons vegan Worcestershire sauce

½ cup frozen peas

¼ cup all-purpose flour

1 sheet vegan puff pastry dough, thawed

2 teaspoons vegan butter, melted

FOR THE MUSHROOM GRAVY

2 tablespoons olive oil

2 cups stemmed and chopped assorted mushrooms (such as cremini and shiitake)

½ cup minced shallots

¼ teaspoon salt

⅛ teaspoon freshly ground black pepper

½ cup dry Marsala wine

1½ cups vegan beef-style broth

1½ tablespoons chopped fresh rosemary

1½ tablespoons all-purpose flour

3 tablespoons vegan butter

TO MAKE THE "BEEF" WELLINGTON

1. Preheat the oven to 400°F.

2. Into a large skillet over medium-high heat, crumble the vegan ground beef. Add the mushrooms, onion, and carrots. Cook for 5 minutes, stirring frequently, until the "beef" is browned. Season with the rosemary, thyme, salt, and black pepper. Add the garlic and cook for 1 minute more.

3. Add the broth and Worcestershire, turn down the heat to low, and simmer for 5 minutes, until most of the liquid is cooked off. Remove from the heat and stir in the frozen peas.

4. Transfer the mixture to a large bowl. Add the flour and stir to fully distribute. The mixture will be thick. Set aside.

5. On a lightly floured surface, roll out the puff pastry into a rectangle. Shape the filling into a loaf and place it lengthwise in the center of the puff pastry.

6. Working from the center out, cut the exposed dough into 1-inch-wide strips. Lay the strips in a crisscross pattern over the filling. Fold the ends of the dough underneath. Lightly brush the surface of the Wellington with the melted butter. Place in a roasting pan.

7. Bake for 30 minutes, until the puff pastry is golden in color. Lightly cover with aluminum foil during the last 10 minutes of baking to prevent excess browning. Let the Wellington stand for 10 minutes, then slice and serve with the mushroom gravy.

TO MAKE THE MUSHROOM GRAVY

8. In a medium skillet over medium-high heat, heat the olive oil. When the oil is hot, add the mushrooms and shallots. Season with the salt and black pepper. Cook for 5 minutes, stirring frequently, until softened.

9. Add the wine and continue cooking for 2 minutes more, until most of the liquid has evaporated. Stir in the broth and rosemary. Whisk in the flour until smooth. Bring to a boil, then turn down the heat to low. Simmer for 10 minutes, stirring occasionally, until thickened slightly. Remove from the heat and stir in the butter until melted into the gravy. Adjust the seasoning to taste with salt and pepper.

Per Serving: Calories: 757; Fat: 42g; Carbohydrates: 60g; Protein: 28g; Fiber: 9g; Sodium: 1,002mg

"Cheesesteak"-Stuffed Peppers

I actually had my first bite of a cheesesteak in Philadelphia, of all places. I was sitting outside for lunch at a tiny sidewalk table, and that's where I fell in love with the combination of fresh ingredients. I've heard it said that a true Philly cheesesteak doesn't include mushrooms or peppers, but I like them, so they're included here. You can simply omit them if you prefer. These vegan stuffed peppers are intended to honor the spirit of the cheesesteak.

3 large bell peppers, any color, stemmed, seeded, and halved lengthwise

2 tablespoons olive oil

2 tablespoons vegan butter

18 ounces vegan beef tips

4 cups stemmed and sliced cremini mushrooms

1 cup diced yellow onion

1 tablespoon steak seasoning blend

1½ cups shredded vegan provolone cheese, divided

1. Preheat the oven to 400°F.

2. In a baking dish, arrange the bell peppers, cut-side up. Bake for 10 minutes, to soften slightly. Discard any liquid that may have accumulated in the bell peppers. Leave the oven on.

3. In a large skillet over medium heat, heat the oil and butter. When the butter is melted, add the vegan beef tips. Cook for 10 minutes, turning frequently, until browned. Transfer to a cutting board and cut into thin slices. Set aside.

4. Into the skillet, add the mushrooms and onion. Cook for 3 minutes, stirring frequently, until softened. Add the vegan beef tip slices and season with the steak seasoning. Continue cooking for 2 minutes more, stirring frequently. Remove from the heat and stir in 1 cup of cheese.

5. Spoon the filling into the bell peppers and top with the remaining ½ cup of cheese. Bake for 15 minutes, then serve.

Per Serving: Calories: 581; Fat: 32g; Carbohydrates: 33g; Protein: 34g; Fiber: 4g; Sodium: 1,744mg

Bruschetta "Chicken" Bake

PREP TIME: 5 minutes

COOK TIME: 40 minutes

SERVES 4 TO 6

The beauty of this casserole is in its simplicity. It comes together in a snap, tastes great, and requires nothing more than an easy salad or roasted broccoli to round out the meal.

Nonstick cooking spray

20 ounces vegan chicken-style strips

½ cup Italian dressing

1 tablespoon olive oil

6 ounces herb-seasoned stuffing mix

1 (14-ounce) can diced tomatoes, with juices

½ cup water

1 tablespoon minced fresh basil

2 teaspoons minced garlic

1 cup shredded vegan mozzarella cheese

1 teaspoon Italian seasoning

Balsamic vinegar, for serving (optional)

1. Preheat the oven to 400°F. Spray a 9-by-13-inch baking dish with cooking spray.

2. In a large bowl, combine the vegan chicken strips and Italian dressing and toss to coat.

3. In a large, deep skillet over medium-high heat, heat the olive oil. When the oil is hot, add the strips, shaking off any excess dressing. Cook for 5 minutes, turning frequently, until browned. Transfer the strips to a cutting board and cut into 1-inch pieces.

4. In a medium bowl, combine the "chicken," stuffing mix, tomatoes with their juices, water, basil, and garlic. Stir gently, just enough to lightly coat all the stuffing mix.

5. Pour the mixture into the prepared baking dish. Sprinkle with the cheese and Italian seasoning.

6. Bake for 30 minutes, until the stuffing is lightly crisp. Drizzle lightly with balsamic vinegar (if using) and serve.

Per Serving: Calories: 514; Fat: 29g; Carbohydrates: 25g; Protein: 39g; Fiber: 8g; Sodium: 1,569mg

Baked "Chicken" Satay

PREP TIME: 15 minutes, plus 1 hour to marinate

COOK TIME: 25 minutes

SERVES 4 TO 6

My daughter's nine-year-old carnivore friend wandered into the kitchen just as these skewers were coming out of the oven and asked for a taste. She took one bite and said, "I thought you guys didn't eat meat." That's when I blew her mind by explaining that it was vegan. She responded, "Wait. You can make meat *from plants?!*"

1½ cups unsweetened coconut milk, divided

¼ cup plus 2 tablespoons brown sugar

2 tablespoons tamari

2 tablespoons freshly squeezed lime juice

1 tablespoon plus 1 teaspoon minced garlic

3½ teaspoons curry seasoning blend, divided

20 ounces crispy vegan chicken pieces

12 (6-inch) skewers

¼ cup creamy peanut butter

⅓ cup vegan chicken-style broth

1 teaspoon chili garlic sauce

1 teaspoon grated fresh ginger

1. In a medium bowl, combine 1 cup of coconut milk, ¼ cup of brown sugar, the tamari, lime juice, garlic, and 2 teaspoons of curry seasoning blend. Add the vegan chicken and toss to coat. Cover and marinate for 1 hour.

2. Preheat the oven to 425°F. Line a baking sheet with parchment paper. If using wooden skewers, soak them in water while the vegan chicken is marinating.

3. Thread the marinated vegan chicken onto skewers, then place them on the prepared baking sheet. Bake for 20 minutes, turning halfway through the cooking time.

4. While the "chicken" is baking, in a small saucepan over medium-high heat, combine the remaining ½ cup of coconut milk, peanut butter, broth, remaining 2 tablespoons of brown sugar, remaining 1½ teaspoons of curry seasoning blend, chili garlic sauce, and ginger. Bring to a low boil, then turn down the heat to low and simmer for 5 minutes, stirring frequently until the sauce is thickened.

5. Arrange the baked chicken satay skewers on a plate and serve warm with the peanut dipping sauce.

Per Serving: Calories: 647; Fat: 44g; Carbohydrates: 27g; Protein: 40g; Fiber: 7g; Sodium: 1,575mg

Tater Tot Casserole

Kids and adults alike love this "meat and potatoes" casserole. It's quick and easy to make with no fussy ingredients required.

Nonstick cooking spray

28 ounces vegan ground beef

½ cup diced yellow onion

½ teaspoon salt

½ teaspoon freshly ground
  black pepper

2 tablespoons all-purpose flour

1 cup vegan beef-style broth

¼ cup mild-flavored plant
  milk (such as oat or
  unsweetened almond)

1 tablespoon vegan
  Worcestershire sauce

2 cups shredded vegan
  Cheddar cheese

32 ounces frozen tater tots

1. Preheat the oven to 400°F. Spray a 9-by-13-inch baking dish with cooking spray.

2. Into a large skillet over medium-high heat, crumble the vegan ground beef, using a spatula to break it up. Add the onion, salt, and pepper. Cook for 5 minutes, stirring frequently, until browned.

3. Sprinkle the "meat" with the flour and stir to evenly distribute. Stir in the broth, milk, and Worcestershire. Cook for 2 minutes, stirring occasionally, until thickened.

4. Spread the "beef" mixture in an even layer in the prepared baking dish. Sprinkle with the cheese, then arrange the tater tots to cover completely.

5. Bake for 30 minutes, then serve.

Per Serving: Calories: 724; Fat: 21g; Carbohydrates: 73g; Protein: 60g; Fiber: 14g; Sodium: 1,920mg

PREP TIME: 20 minutes

COOK TIME: 1 hour
30 minutes

SERVES 4

"Sausage"-Stuffed Baked Potatoes

Baked potatoes are no longer just an everyday side dish. These twice-baked potatoes are a meal unto themselves. The combination of vegan bratwurst and sauerkraut gives a nice German-style flair that I like, especially around Oktoberfest season.

4 large russet potatoes

1 tablespoon olive oil

½ teaspoon salt, plus more for seasoning

¼ teaspoon freshly ground black pepper, plus more for seasoning

2 vegan bratwurst sausage links, cut into ¼-inch slices

1 cup thinly sliced yellow onion

½ cup lager beer

⅓ cup vegan butter

1 cup shredded vegan mozzarella cheese

½ cup sauerkraut, well drained

1. Preheat the oven to 400°F.

2. Lightly coat the potatoes with the olive oil and sprinkle generously with the salt and black pepper. Bake for 1 hour or until the potatoes are easily pierced with a fork. Set the potatoes aside until they are cool enough to handle. Switch the oven setting to broil.

3. Slice each potato across the top lengthwise, leaving enough flesh that the skin retains its shape, about ¼ inch. Scoop out the flesh of each potato and place in a medium bowl. Set aside.

4. In a medium skillet over medium-high heat, put the vegan sausage slices in an even layer. Cook for 6 minutes, turning frequently, until browned. Transfer the cooked sausage slices to a cutting board. Do not wipe out the skillet. Roughly chop the sausage into small pieces.

5. Turn down the heat to medium, then add the sliced onions to the skillet. Season with salt and black pepper. Cook for 20 minutes, stirring frequently, until the onions are caramelized to a golden-brown color.

6. Into the skillet with the onions, add the chopped sausage and lager beer. Stir frequently for 1 minute while the beer reduces slightly.

7. Add the vegan butter, mozzarella, and sausage-onion mixture to the bowl with the potato. Stir gently to combine and adjust the seasoning with salt and black pepper to taste.

8. Spoon the filling into the scooped-out potato skins in heaping amounts. Place the filled potatoes on a baking sheet and place under the broiler for 2 minutes, just until lightly browned.

9. To serve, top each potato with sauerkraut and a sprinkle of black pepper.

Per Serving: Calories: 567; Fat: 22g; Carbohydrates: 79g; Protein: 14g; Fiber: 6g; Sodium: 836mg

Loaded "Chicken" Nachos

PREP TIME: 10 minutes

COOK TIME: 20 minutes

SERVES 4

My dad used to love making nachos for dinner. Chips and cheese only, though; my dad was a purist and, man, did I ever love nacho night. Dad would come out of the kitchen and plop the scalding-hot baking sheet right down in the middle of the table and we all would huddle around vying for the best, cheesiest chips. Nacho night has continued at my house but as a more well-rounded, vegan meal. I think Dad would approve.

1 tablespoon vegetable oil

10 ounces vegan chicken-style strips

¼ cup sliced scallions

1 cup black beans, drained and rinsed

1 tablespoon taco seasoning

½-pound bag tortilla chips

3 cups shredded vegan cheese of your choice, divided

1 cup vegan refried beans

Salsa, for topping (optional)

Guacamole, for topping (optional)

Black olives, for topping (optional)

Pickled or fresh jalapeño pepper slices, for topping (optional)

Shredded lettuce, for topping (optional)

Red onion slices, for topping (optional)

Vegan sour cream, for topping (optional)

1. Preheat the oven to 350°F.

2. In a large skillet over medium-high heat, heat the vegetable oil. When the oil is hot, add the vegan chicken strips. Cook for 5 minutes, turning frequently, until browned. Transfer the cooked strips to a cutting board and roughly chop. Set aside.

3. Into the skillet, add the scallions, black beans, and taco seasoning. Stir to combine and cook for 2 minutes to heat through. Add the chopped vegan chicken to the skillet and stir to incorporate.

4. On a large baking sheet, spread out the tortilla chips. Sprinkle with 1 cup of cheese. Spoon the refried beans onto the chips, then top with the vegan chicken and bean mixture. Sprinkle with the remaining 2 cups of cheese.

5. Bake the nachos for 10 minutes, until the cheese is melted and the chips are starting to brown around the edges. Pile on any additional desired toppings and dig in!

Per Serving: Calories: 995; Fat: 49g; Carbohydrates: 82g; Protein: 56g; Fiber: 13g; Sodium: 2,123mg

MEASUREMENT CONVERSIONS

VOLUME EQUIVALENTS	U.S. STANDARD	U.S. STANDARD (ounces)	METRIC (approximate)
LIQUID	2 tablespoons	1 fl. oz.	30 mL
	¼ cup	2 fl. oz.	60 mL
	½ cup	4 fl. oz.	120 mL
	1 cup	8 fl. oz.	240 mL
	1½ cups	12 fl. oz.	355 mL
	2 cups or 1 pint	16 fl. oz.	475 mL
	4 cups or 1 quart	32 fl. oz.	1 L
	1 gallon	128 fl. oz.	4 L
DRY	⅛ teaspoon	—	0.5 mL
	¼ teaspoon	—	1 mL
	½ teaspoon	—	2 mL
	¾ teaspoon	—	4 mL
	1 teaspoon	—	5 mL
	1 tablespoon	—	15 mL
	¼ cup	—	59 mL
	⅓ cup	—	79 mL
	½ cup	—	118 mL
	⅔ cup	—	156 mL
	¾ cup	—	177 mL
	1 cup	—	235 mL
	2 cups or 1 pint	—	475 mL
	3 cups	—	700 mL
	4 cups or 1 quart	—	1 L
	½ gallon	—	2 L
	1 gallon	—	4 L

OVEN TEMPERATURES

FAHRENHEIT	CELSIUS (approximate)
250°F	120°C
300°F	150°C
325°F	165°C
350°F	180°C
375°F	190°C
400°F	200°C
425°F	220°C
450°F	230°C

WEIGHT EQUIVALENTS

U.S. STANDARD	METRIC (approximate)
½ ounce	15 g
1 ounce	30 g
2 ounces	60 g
4 ounces	115 g
8 ounces	225 g
12 ounces	340 g
16 ounces or 1 pound	455 g

REFERENCES

Food Industry Executive. "Plant-Based Meat Market Size Worth $35.4 Billion by 2027." July 28, 2020. https://foodindustryexecutive.com/2020/07 /plant-based-meat-market-size-worth-35-4-billion-by-2027-cagr-15-8/.

Gelsomin, Emily, MLA, RD, LDN. "Impossible and Beyond: How Healthy Are These Meatless Burgers?" *Harvard Health Blog*. August 15, 2019. https://www.health.harvard.edu/blog/impossible-and-beyond-how -healthy-are-these-meatless-burgers-2019081517448.

Hoekstra, Arjen Y. "The Hidden Water Resource Use Behind Meat and Dairy." *Animal Frontiers* vol. 2, no. 2: 3–8. April 2012. https://waterfootprint.org /media/downloads/Hoekstra-2012-Water-Meat-Dairy_1.pdf.

Jordan, Rennie. "Greenpeace Recommends 50 Percent Reduction in Meat and Dairy Consumption by 2050." Foodtank. June 2018. https://foodtank.com /news/2018/06/greenpeace-report-reduce-meat-dairy-consumption/.

Moore, Andrew, MD (Ed.). "Food Allergy." *American Academy of Allergy Asthma & Immunology*. September 28, 2020. https://www.aaaai.org /Tools-for-the-Public/Conditions-Library/Allergies/Food-Allergy-TTR.

People for the Ethical Treatment of Animals. "Meat and the Environment." Accessed June 8, 2021. https://www.peta.org/issues/animals-used-for-food /meat-environment/.

People for the Ethical Treatment of Animals. "Your Guide to Soy- and Gluten-Free Meatless Meat." Accessed June 8, 2021. https://www.peta.org/living/food /guide-soy-gluten-free-meatless-meat/.

Turney, Spencer. "Behavioral Science Models Can Help Identify the Greenest Dietary Changes." *Vanderbilt News.* August 9, 2019. https://news .vanderbilt.edu/2019/08/09/behavioral-science-models-can-help-identify -the-greenest-dietary-changes/.

United States Environmental Protection Agency. "Sources of Greenhouse Gas Emissions." Accessed June 8, 2021. https://www.epa.gov/ghgemissions /sources-greenhouse-gas-emissions#agriculture.

INDEX

Acknowledgments

To my wonderful husband, Harry Gray, thank you for believing in me and encouraging me to pursue my passions all while enduring countless hours of taste testing and weeks on end of Thanksgiving-level dish washing. Your unwavering support has been instrumental in turning my dream of publishing a cookbook into reality. I love you.

Gurvinder Gandu and the team at Callisto Media, thank you for a positive publishing experience. Collaborating with you on this project has been delightful and educational. Thank you for choosing to work with me.

Finally, thank you to the readers of my blog, *This Wife Cooks*, along with the legions of chefs, home cooks, and fellow foodies out there who continuously inspire me to learn and create.

About the Author

 Holly V. Gray is creator of the vegan food blog *This Wife Cooks*. Her work has been featured in *VegNews* magazine, *The Washington Post*, and various other publications in print and online.

She lives in northern Virginia.

Facebook, Instagram, and Twitter: @ThisWifeCooks

CPSIA information can be obtained
at www.ICGtesting.com
Printed in the USA
JSHW011504210721
17116JS00002B/2